THE POWER OF
SELF

MASTER
TEACHINGS

The Path to Self-mastery, Vol 1

THE POWER OF

SELF

A practical guide to knowing the Self

KIM MICHAELS

Copyright © 2013 Kim Michaels. All rights reserved.

No part of this book may be reproduced, translated or transmitted by any means except by written permission from the publisher. A reviewer may quote brief passages in a review.

For information and foreign rights, contact:

MORE TO LIFE PUBLISHING,

Website: www.morepublish.com

E-mail: info@morepublish.com

Hardcover ISBN: 978–9949–9383–8–4

Series ISBN: 978–9949–9383–4–6

Cover and interior design: Helen Michaels

Notes and disclaimers: (1) No guarantee is made by the author or the publisher that the practices described in this book will yield successful results for anyone at any time. They are presented for informational purposes only, as the practice and proof rests with the individual. (2) The information and insights in this book are solely the opinion of the author and should not be considered as a form of therapy, advice, direction, diagnosis and/or treatment of any kind. This information is not a substitute for medical, psychological, or other professional advice, counseling, or care. All matters pertaining to your individual health should be supervised by a physician or appropriate health-care practitioner. Neither the author nor the publisher assumes any responsibility or liability whatsoever on behalf of any purchaser or reader.

CONTENTS

Introduction | "Why should I read this book?" — 13
   The central human enigma — 14
   A life-changing shift — 15
   Your are more than your current self — 16
   How the self limits you — 16
   The enigma of personal growth — 17

PART ONE - A frame of reference
from outside the human perception filter

Chapter 1 | Science and the power of Self — 21
   Looking for hidden causes — 22
   Mind over matter — 23
   A world beyond the material — 25
   The quantum measurement enigma — 26
   No thing is separate — 28
   The uncertainty enigma — 29
   A self-empowering world view — 30
   An interconnected whole — 33
   How pure energy becomes matter — 35
   The Universe after the Big Bang — 37
   Our higher and lower potential — 38
   How the world was created — 39

Chapter 2 | How the ascended masters can help you — 41
   What kind of teacher do you want? — 42
   Our universal teachers — 44
   You are ready for a higher teaching — 45
   What is an ascended master? — 47
   Why have you never heard about ascended masters? — 48

Why is there no proof that the masters exist?	49
Why are the masters important?	50
Why do ascended masters care about us?	51
The purpose of the world of form	53
Ascended masters and the power of Self	54
Two ways to change our lives	56

Chapter 3 | Are the ascended masters real? — 58

A mystical approach to objectivity	59
The kaleidoscope of the mind	61
The essence of mysticism	63
Why is the mystical approach so important?	64

Chapter 4 | How the world of form was created — 67

The hierarchical structure of the universe	67
What is beyond the world of form	68
How our world was created	69
The creation of self-aware beings	71
The succession of spheres	73
Introducing spiritual rays	75
Four levels of the world	77
We are extensions of the masters	78

PART TWO - A practical approach to spiritual growth

Chapter 5 | Fundamental questions about self — 81

Who am I? What is the Self?	81
Where did the Self come from?	82
What is my relationship with GOD?	84
Where am I going; what happens after death?	85
Why is reincarnation important	87

Chapter 6 | How to anchor yourself firmly on the path — 88

The initial trial period	89

The two "legs" of the path	90
The importance of invoking light	92
The mass consciousness	93
Understanding dark forces	95
Invocations and decrees	97
A practical program	99
1.01 Decree to Archangel Michael	102
4.01 Decree to Elohim Astrea	104
7.03 Decree to Saint Germain	106

PART THREE - *Knowing the Self and its components*

Chapter 7 | Mastering your reactions	110
The essential key to self-mastery	112
Chapter 8 | The Self in the spiritual realm	115
The inherent risk factor	117
Understanding your higher self	119
The two aspects of your I AM Presence	123
Chapter 9 | The Self that descends into the material world	126
Creating a Self that cannot be lost	127
Knowing through a mystical experience: Gnosis	128
How does the Self express itself?	131
Why has the Self forgotten who it is?	132
Questioning the perception filter	134
Dismantling the perception filters	136
How we create a limited self here on earth	139
Chapter 10 | The "self" that is created in the material world	142
How the Conscious You descended	144
Why the soul cannot ascend	146
The container of self and your four lower bodies	149
How you lost contact with your spiritual self	151

Chapter 11 | Escaping the prison of the ego	155
The levels of the ego	157
The Subconscious mind	162
Creating a computer program	162
The way out	164
Transcending subconscious programs	165
How the ego complicates the process	169
The body mind	170
Chapter 12 | Other aspects of the Self	173
Your causal body	173
Your Christ self	176
A gradual path	178

PART FOUR - *A closer look at the spiritual path*

Chapter 13 | Choosing to shift your Life Experience	183
Why you are here right now	184
The shift can happen instantly	186
Immersion and awakening experiences	187
Chapter 14 | An ascended master perspective on karma	191
Physical karma	193
Mind karma	195
Getting out of a karmic hole	197
The cause of karma	198
No automatic way to balance karma	199
Karma and the seven rays	201
Your Divine plan	202
The ascension: the ultimate goal	205
Chapter 15 | Understanding why you need the ascended masters	209
Understanding how beings start the path	210

The ideal scenario	211
Understanding the forbidden fruit and the fall of man	212
Understanding the subtlety of the serpentine logic	216
How the fall happened	218
A closer look at the serpentine mind	221
What type of experiences do you want?	222
Earth is below the ideal scenario	225
Walking the spiritual path today	226

PART FIVE - *Introducing the seven rays*

Chapter 16 | Introduction to the Seven Rays	231
The characteristics of a ray	232
The rays and the chakras	233
Spiritual retreats	235
Introducing the First Ray	236
Introducing the Second Ray	238
Introducing the Third Ray	239
Introducing the Fourth Ray	241
Introducing the Fifth Ray	243
Introducing the Sixth Ray	245
Introducing the Seventh Ray	247
About the Author	249

INTRODUCTION

"WHY SHOULD I READ THIS BOOK?"

In the modern world we spend less time making a living than previous generations and we have all kinds of technological devices that are designed to save us time. Yet most of us still feel we never have enough time. So why would you want to take time from your busy schedule to read this book?

Well, the simple answer is that you want to read this book because you are ready for it. You are ready to rise to the next level of your personal path, and this book will show you how to get there. How can I know you are ready for this book? Consider this simple law:

When the student is ready, the teacher appears.

If you had not been ready for this book, you would not have found it and thus you would not be reading these words. Your outer mind may have objections to this statement, and your outer mind may have objections to some of the things you will read in this book. Yet at a deeper level of your being, you know that you are ready to ascend to a higher approach to the process we call life. And this book will present you with a gradual path to unlock the power you already have inside of you, the power of Self.

There is another factor that shows you are ready for this book. This book fits into the categories of self-help, self-improvement, self-empowerment and spirituality. Given that there are thousands of books in these genres, it is likely that you have already read one or several books about

-Introduction

how to improve your life. You might have read about 48 laws, 33 initiations, 24 keys, 12 steps, 10 insights, 7 habits, 4 agreements or 1 secret.

So given that you have already read about this topic, yet you have still picked up another book, what does this tell you? It tells you that you did not get the results you wanted from the other books. If you had gotten those results, you would be enjoying a new life. And why would you be reading another book telling you how to get somewhere if you were already there?

So what might this book do for you that the other books didn't do? Well, to be perfectly honest, this book will do nothing for you—no book ever could. What this book will do is to show you how you can do something for yourself by using the power you already have inside of you. And the very fact that you have found this book shows you that – in the inner recesses of your being – you are ready for this approach. I know this will at first seem to be of little help, but things will clear up after we look at the human enigma.

THE CENTRAL HUMAN ENIGMA

Right now, you experience that your life is defined by certain limitations. You would like to go beyond those limitations, but you feel powerless to do so on your own. After all, if you had the power to get beyond your limitations, you would have already done so and thus have no need to read a book about it. So when a book tells you that you do have the power within yourself to solve your problems, it can at first seem like a slap in the face. And this is what we might call the central human enigma.

The human enigma is simply this: You experience that you are limited by certain external circumstances. You experience that you do not have the power to change them—or you would already have done so. So how can you possibly break free of this prison, how can you solve the enigma? How can you change your life unless some external savior comes in and does for you what you obviously cannot do for yourself? And this, of course, is what sets many people on a quest to find this external savior or secret formula.

Yet after you have been on this quest and gotten nowhere, there comes a point, where you become open to the deeper truth that can actually resolve the human enigma. And again, if you were not open to this truth, you would not be reading these words.

What is the deeper truth? Well, it is that your experience is perfectly correct. You are indeed limited by certain circumstances that you do not have the power to change. Yet the *only* reason you do not have power to change them is that you are looking at life through one particular self. And that self is *not* the only possible way to look at life.

A LIFE-CHANGING SHIFT

The fact that you have found this book shows that you are ready to make a fundamental shift in consciousness. What is that shift? If you believe and experience that you are limited by external circumstances, you will inevitably think that the only way to change your life, your Life Experience, is to find a way to change something outside yourself. Yet the next phase is that you redirect your attention, so that instead of focusing on what is happening outside yourself, you focus on your Self.

The realization that can solve the human enigma is that there is more than one kind of self. Right now you have a specific sense of self, a specific sense of identity. Yet this self is not real and it is not the real you. It is simply a filter through which you are looking at the world.

The simplest possible illustration is that if you put on colored glasses, the world seems to have a certain tint. Yet you know that the world has not been changed by you putting on glasses—what has changed is the way you look at the world. Likewise, the way you look at life right now is a product of your sense of self. So do you actually live in a world where you are limited by external circumstances? Or are the limitations a product of the way you look at the world through the filter of self?

-Introduction

YOU ARE MORE THAN YOUR CURRENT SELF

The simple, yet ultimately liberating, realization is that you are *not* your current sense of self. You are *more* than your current sense of self, and this book will explain exactly what that means. It is perfectly true that as long as you look through the perception filter of your current sense of self, you will not be able to solve your current problems. As Albert Einstein said: "You cannot solve a problem with the same state of consciousness that created the problem." Yet what you really need to see is that you cannot overcome a limitation by using the very sense of self that defined that limitation and made it seem real.

So what is the key to overcoming the human enigma? How do you change the equation, which says you cannot solve your problems by your own power and that you cannot find an external savior to do it for you? The key is to realize that you have an option that you were never told about in school or Sunday school. And that option is to deliberately and consciously change your sense of self.

The entire purpose of this book is to give you the knowledge and the practical tools to shift your sense of self. Yet the book will do this by showing you what the self really is—because unless you know the Self, how can you unlock the power of Self?

HOW THE SELF LIMITS YOU

I have been on the path of self-transcendence for a while, and I have observed thousands of people struggle with the same issues that I have dealt with. In my observation, there are two distinct phases on the path. The first one is the phase where we are focused on changing something outside ourselves, and the second phase is where we make a shift and focus on changing what is inside ourselves. And again, if you were not ready to make that shift, why would you be reading this?

So the first realization that forms the basis for this book is that you need to shift your sense of self. The second realization is that in order

The Power of Self

to shift your sense of self, you need to have a point of reference from outside yourself. Why is that so important?

Have you ever read the fairy tale about the emperor's new clothes? The short version is that an emperor hires a crew of tailors to make him the fanciest clothes ever. Yet the tailors are not actually making a set of clothes; they are simply making the emperor and his court believe they are making the clothes. And because they are all inside the "perception filter" created by the tailors, no one can see that the emperor is stark naked. Even when the emperor parades in front of his people, they all buy into the illusion—until a little boy finally utters the timeless words: "But the emperor's got nothing on!"

The simple fact is that your current sense of self forms a perception filter that colors the way you see everything. And how will you escape the illusion, unless you receive some impulse from outside the mental box of your current self, something that makes you ask a simple question: "Is the way I look at the world accurate, or is there more to life than what I can see right now?"

Yet do you see the fundamental truth here? As long as you are wearing colored glasses, everything you see will be colored by the glasses. Which means that nothing you see through the glasses will enable you to question your perception. So the first step towards changing your sense of self is that you must have some point of reference, which allows you to begin to question what you see through the filter of your self.

What this book will do for you is to take you through a process that will challenge the way you have been brought up to look at life. You can only shift your sense of self by questioning the perception of life that you receive through your current sense of self. And this brings up the final point I want to get across in this introduction.

THE ENIGMA OF PERSONAL GROWTH

Self-transcendence presents an inescapable challenge. As I have said, somewhere inside of you, there is a longing for something more, even a sense that it is possible for you to find a better approach to life. The key

-Introduction

to fulfilling this inner longing is to shift your sense of self. Yet your current self will not simply roll over and die just because you start reading this book.

I have talked about stepping up to a higher stage, where you no longer focus on changing what is outside yourself but focus on changing your sense of self. Yet it is a simple fact that your current self will resist this shift. It will want you to continue focusing on everything else, and the reason is that it has a certain survival instinct.

The result of this is that when we step up to the higher phase of consciously changing our sense of self, we will at first feel like we are being pulled in opposite directions. We can feel like the rope in a tug-of-war, being pulled by two teams. This leads to a phase that is somewhat turbulent, because as you begin to question the perception of your old self, you will feel like you can no longer believe what you used to think was infallible truths. You will feel like you are not quite sure what is real or who you are, and there will be a voice inside of you screaming that this is dangerous and that you must go back to the old sense of self in order to avoid a major calamity.

This book will show you a gradual and gentle path to get through this stage and truly transcend the old self while finding your real self. Yet, again, the book cannot do it for you. What will help you is to realize that you will have to go through this initial stage of questioning your current perception and allowing some of your cherished beliefs and opinions to be challenged. And you will make this process much easier for yourself by deciding to keep an eye on your own reactions.

As you read this book, monitor your reactions to the ideas it presents. When you find that you have an unusually strong reaction to an idea, you will know that you have now uncovered one of the unexamined beliefs that block your personal progress. Your current self is presenting you with a certain perception of life, and your current self believes it is not a perception but reality. So what you need to do is to realize it is just a perception and to continue questioning it until you see how it limits you. Once you see how this particular belief stops the power of Self from flowing through you, you will instantly let it go and shift into a higher sense of self.

Hopefully you will have many breakthrough experiences as you read the book and apply the tools it presents. This book truly presents a practical path that can shift your sense of self in a surprisingly short period of time. If you go through the process with an awareness of the two voices – one wanting you to let go and the other wanting you to cling to your current self – you will one day look back and be amazed at how much your world view has shifted and how much more free and empowered you feel. So let us get on with challenging the perception filter of your current self, seeking to free the real you to manifest the life you want.

PART ONE

A FRAME OF REFERENCE FROM OUTSIDE THE HUMAN PERCEPTION FILTER

CHAPTER 1

SCIENCE AND THE POWER OF SELF

Obviously, you are not currently able to express the power of Self, or you would be enjoying a new life instead of reading this. The conclusion is that your power is being blocked, and what is blocking it is not external limitations but your own perception of life. This perception makes certain limitations seem real, yet this is simply a product of your current sense of self.

So the key to unlocking the power of Self is to shift your sense of self by challenging the perception of life that you get through your current sense of self. And the key to challenging your current mental box is to get a point of reference from outside the box. You need to have an alternative view in order to question the world view presented by your current perception filter. So the question becomes: How far outside your current mental box are you willing to go?

The simple fact is that most of us have come to accept a world view that is very disempowering and causes us to shut off almost all of the power of Self. In order to completely unlock the power of self, we have to make a very dramatic shift in our world view and sense of self. None of us can make that shift in one move, so we all need to take a gradual path.

This book will present you with a frame of reference that can take you completely beyond the human mental box. Yet in order to give you a gentle start, I would like to deal with what we might call the fundamental issue of self-help. The basic idea behind self-help is that you can change

| 1 | *Science and the Power of Self*

your life by changing your attitude or state of mind. Yet we have all been brought up with a world view that makes this claim seem impossible. After all, our senses and common experience – perhaps even our belief systems – tell us that our minds do not have power over matter.

So what I will do in this chapter is to take a look at how some of the discoveries of science can help us challenge the seeming disconnect between mind and matter.

LOOKING FOR HIDDEN CAUSES

Let us look at a simplified example. Say you are sitting at a table and on the table is a ball. How can you move that ball from Point A to Point B? Can you make the ball roll by using the powers of your mind to move the ball directly? Or will you have to use indirect power, by getting your mind to move your hand, so that the material object of your hand moves the material object of the ball?

If you think about this, you will see that the way you look at the problem depends on how you answer another question: "Is the ball separate from the mind or is there a connection between them?" If you believe that the ball and the mind are separate with no connection between them, then obviously there is no way your mind can directly move the ball. If the mind is made of one substance and the ball is made of a fundamentally different kind of stuff, then mind stuff simply cannot change matter stuff.

Yet what does modern science say about this? You might have read that science began in the Middle Ages, when most people believed the earth was the center of the universe. By observing the actual movements of heavenly objects, scientists discovered that the earth was moving around the sun. So let us look at some other observations of science and see what they can tell us about mind and matter.

We can begin by realizing that the idea that the earth was the center of the universe was quite reasonable based on our sensory perception. After all, our eyes tell us that the sun is moving across the sky, because our senses cannot see that the earth is rotating on its axis. Why can't our senses tell us this? Since we are moving with the earth, they have no frame of reference from outside the earth. So the first lesson from science is that we cannot trust our senses, meaning we have to reach for something from outside the perception filter of our physical senses.

Science has also shown us that we live in a world that has layers or levels. What we can see with our senses is only a surface layer of the world, what scientists call the macroscopic level. Yet science has abundantly proven that there is something beyond the macroscopic level. What we see as human bodies, mountains or toasters are all made from smaller building blocks, called molecules. And molecules are made from even smaller blocks, called atoms, which are made from smaller blocks, called elementary particles.

The next insight given by science is the concept of cause and effect. In some cases, there is an obvious cause-effect relationship at the macroscopic level. If my hand pushes the ball, then that is obviously the cause of the ball moving. Yet in many cases, we can understand the cause behind visible phenomena only by looking at a deeper or higher level of the world. We can see many different things on earth, but at a deeper level they are all made of atoms. So the form that things can take and the way they behave is to some extent an effect of causes at the atomic level. And as we shall see shortly, there are even deeper levels of the world than atoms.

Another important realization demonstrated by science is that what seems like a bewildering display of diversity to our senses is actually just an appearance. When you go beyond the macroscopic level, we find less and less diversity the deeper or higher we go. There are millions of different things on earth, but they are all made from just 108 atoms. And the atoms are made by combining just three types of elementary particles in different ways.

MIND OVER MATTER

All of the factors mentioned so far are sort of common sense, and they can be deduced from what we all learned in elementary school. They

| 1 | *Science and the Power of Self*

simply prove the necessity of looking beyond the perception filter of our sensory-based macroscopic world view. Yet science can actually help us go even further beyond that mental box.

The first earth-shattering challenge to the sensory-based world view came in 1905 when Albert Einstein published the theory of relativity. When I went to school, my physics teacher told me that the world was made from two elements: matter and energy. I was, of course, told about the theory of relativity, yet what I learned was still based on the dualistic view of a world made from two elements. For example, I was told that Einstein's formula, $E=mc^2$, explains how we can convert matter into energy by splitting the atom. I am guessing you were taught something similar.

It was only after I grew up that I learned what Einstein's formula truly says. You can begin to understand this by asking yourself why it is possible to convert matter into energy? Why is it, that when we split the atom, huge quantities of energy are released? The simple answer is that splitting the atom does not produce energy that wasn't there—it simply frees the energy that was already inside the atom. Okay, then, but why is there energy inside the atom? Because what Einstein's theory truly says is that everything is made from energy.

Since 1905 we have known that our sensory-based world view is out of touch with reality. What our senses detect as solid matter is not solid at all. Matter is made from energy, and energy is a form of vibration, a wave that is constantly oscillating. What we see as solid and unchangeable matter is simply energy waves that have been captured into a stationary matrix. Yet as nuclear power plants prove, solid matter can be changed back into fluid energy.

Even more important, energy is infinitely changeable. Any energy wave can be changed into any other energy wave by changing its vibrational properties. This means that Einstein actually broke down the barrier between mind and matter. Matter is made from energy waves, and so are thoughts. Based on the theory of relativity it is entirely possible that the human mind can produce an energy wave so powerful, that it can have an effect on the energy waves that are currently making up "solid" matter.

Any solid and unchangeable matter is simply energy waves that have been captured into a stationary matrix.

In other words, self-help – the potential to change your physical circumstances by using the power of the mind – has been a scientific potential since 1905. It has obviously been a real potential much longer than that. Yet science can take us even further beyond the common mental box.

A WORLD BEYOND THE MATERIAL

After Einstein presented his theory of relativity, a group of physicists got very excited, and they decided to study the world inside the atom based on Einstein's discoveries. Over the following decades, they developed a new branch of science, called quantum mechanics, and they have made some truly mind-blowing discoveries.

The first one we will look at is the so-called wave-particle duality. According to a sensory-based view, something has to be either a wave or a particle. Yet physicists have proven that a subatomic "entity" will sometimes behave as a particle and sometimes as a wave. To me this is a clear indication of how important it is to look beyond the macroscopic perception filter.

A simple explanation for the paradox is that a subatomic entity is a more fundamental thing than wave or particle. Yet because physicists have attempted to force a wave-particle perception filter upon the subatomic world, they sometimes get wave properties and sometimes particle properties. It is truly like the emperor's new clothes, where physicists are still so blinded by their perception filter that they cannot see subatomic particles for what they really are.

| 1 | Science and the Power of Self

This might indicate that when physicists study the subatomic world, they are actually on the borderline between the material world and a greater world beyond the material. The "stuff" that makes up this greater world does not yet have form as we conceive of form. It is not yet locked into what we conceive of as a particle or a wave. It has the potential to take on the form of either a particle or a wave, and apparently, the specific form it takes on can be affected by something that we human beings do. If we look for a particle, the "quantum stuff" will behave like one, and if we look for a wave, it will behave like that also.

The conclusion we now reach is that we do not live in a world that is made up of solid, unchangeable particles. We live in a world that is far more fluid or moldable than what we have come to believe. It seems like the world is made from quantum stuff that has no fixed form but can take on any form. And it seems like our minds can influence which form the quantum stuff takes on.

THE QUANTUM MEASUREMENT ENIGMA

When physicists started looking at the subatomic world, they expected that they could do what scientists do in the macroscopic world, namely be objective observers of independent objects. Yet they soon realized that in the quantum world, there is no objective observer—because there are no separate objects. When a physicist uses a particle accelerator to study a subatomic particle, the outcome is not independent of the mind of the scientist. Instead, the outcome is a product of three factors, namely the particle accelerator, the subatomic particle *and* the mind of the scientist. In the subatomic world, there is no such thing as an objective observer. In the subatomic world everything is connected, and the mind of the scientist will have a fundamental and unavoidable influence on the outcome of the experiment.

To make matters worse, physicists also discovered that in the subatomic world the laws of nature, that work so well in the macroscopic world, no longer apply. In the quantum world, the laws of nature simply break down. You can calculate with absolute precision how a rocket moves towards Mars, but you cannot predict the movements of an electron around the nucleus. How can we explain this?

Since I am neither a scientist nor a materialist, I see a relatively simple explanation. To present it, let me go back to Einstein's formula, $E=mc^2$ and the fact that matter is simply another form of energy. Matter is energy that has been captured into a matrix, so that instead of behaving like a non-local wave, it now behaves like a localized "particle."

Once energy has passed this threshold, it forms particles that can be combined into the things we can detect with our senses and most scientific instruments. This is the macroscopic world, and this world is indeed subject to what we call the laws of nature. In the macroscopic world there are things that were not created by the human mind, and thus it is correct that the human mind has no direct influence on such things or the laws of nature.

So how does this fit in with quantum physics? My explanation is that scientists have proven that we live in a world that has layers. Up until the advent of quantum physics, scientists were aware of only one layer, one pocket, of the total world, namely the macroscopic world. The quantum world is not just another part of the macroscopic world; it is a more fundamental layer. That is why the laws of nature break down in the quantum world. That is why there are no separate particles in the quantum world. And that is why the quantum world has a connection between our minds and subatomic so-called particles. Classical physicists said that the world is like a giant machine in which everything is predictable. This clearly is not the case at the quantum level. There are avant-garde physicists who say that the world resembles a giant mind rather than a giant machine. This means that if you truly acknowledge what quantum physics has proven, then you see that science can no longer afford to ignore mind. The final frontier is not space, because the ultimate frontier is consciousness. Of course, that is what self-help and spiritual teachers have been saying all along.

| 1 | Science and the Power of Self

NO THING IS SEPARATE

Given that quantum physicists first proved non-locality several decades ago, why hasn't our world view been adjusted accordingly? I mean, consider what scientists are actually saying. The universe started with the Big Bang, which took place about 15 billion years ago. In the first milliseconds, the laws of nature that we know today did not exist. Some of the first "things" to appear were what we call subatomic particles, so they have been around for a while. It then took 15 billion years before humans appeared, and we were the first beings with sophisticated consciousness. Meaning that between the appearance of subatomic particles and our consciousness, there is an evolutionary distance of 15 billion years—a rather large gap, I would say.

Quantum physicists have now proven that our consciousness can interact with subatomic particles.

Yet quantum physicists have now proven beyond any doubt that our consciousness can interact with subatomic particles, meaning that our very young consciousness can interact with "entities" that are 15 billion years older than we are. How do you explain this? Well, to me the simple explanation is that the world is made from neither matter nor energy. The underlying reality of the world is consciousness.

There was a form of consciousness that was present at the creation of subatomic particles, and that is why our more recent minds can interact with these "particles." Are we actually interacting with separate particles, or are we interacting with the mind that creates and sustains them?

Take note that I am not hereby saying that we need to go back and accept the Judeo-Christian all-male God and the creation of the universe in seven days. I am, however, saying that the simplest explanation for the findings of quantum physics is that the Big Bang was planned and

The Power of Self

executed by a mind larger than ours. Between then and now, there has been a gradual, evolutionary process, but it has not been the random, unconscious process postulated by materialism. It has been a process that has been guided partly by one or more larger minds, partly – at the macroscopic level – by the laws of nature and partly by a third factor. What is this mystery factor? Well, if our minds are able to interact with and shape subatomic particles, what does that say about our potential to shape the macroscopic world? What does it say about why we are here in the first place?

THE UNCERTAINTY ENIGMA

Classical physics says that the entire universe is a machine, like a giant clock. Everything is made from interconnected levers and gears, and they all work according to laws that never vary. The implication of this is that the functioning of the universe is predictable. If you know enough about the universe's starting position and the laws of nature, you can calculate with absolute certainty every event that will ever happen—up until the end of the world.

When physicists began studying the quantum world, they expected to find distinct particles that behaved according to invariable laws, pretty much like miniature billiard balls zooming around on a pool table. Meaning that if you knew enough about a particle, you could predict its behavior with certainty. What they found instead was another enigma that is unthinkable according to a traditional mental box.

In the quantum world, it is fundamentally impossible to predict the movements of a particle, such as an electron. This is not because you don't know enough about the electron, but because there is a fundamental uncertainty in the quantum world. Instead of behaving according to invariable laws, the quantum world is inherently unpredictable. You cannot know the position of an electron until you actually measure it. And even then, what you measure is not an independent electron. What you are actually doing by your measurement is to create an electron in that position. What you measure simply was not there before you made the observation.

There is a form of consciousness present in the quantum world. This explains why our minds can co-create the particles we observe.

Based on what I have said above, we can once again suggest a simple explanation. Science has shown that there must be a form of consciousness present in the quantum world. This is simply the only way to explain why our minds can interact with the quantum reality and co-create the particles we observe. And what is the main characteristic of consciousness, at least for self-aware beings? It is that it does not follow mechanical laws. It has the potential to be creative, to do something that no mind has ever done before. Yet what is the basis for this creativity? It is free will; the ability to imagine something never done before and then choosing to do it for the first time. Okay, now that I have set a foundation, let me sketch a world view that can help you unlock the power of Self.

A SELF-EMPOWERING WORLD VIEW

Those of us who have grown up in the modern world have been brought up with a world view that is a strange mixture of medieval religious concepts, actual scientific observations, concepts that spring from materialism, and our sensory observations. As a result, we have a world view which says the following:

- We live in a world made of matter.
- Matter is "solid," meaning it has substance and continuity.
- Matter is difficult to change.

The Power of Self

- All the things we see in the macroscopic world are made from matter, and these things exist as separate units. We live on a planet that is such a unit. It is affected by the sun, but it is also surrounded by empty space that sets it apart. Our bodies are likewise separate units.
- Matter is separate from mind.
- Our minds have no ability to change matter directly. We can change matter only through our matter bodies and technology based on matter.
- The matter world has power over our minds and sets many limits for our creative abilities.

All of these points are rather disempowering, because they essentially portray us as passive recipients of whatever the external matter world decides to throw at us. Yet based on the findings of quantum physics, we can challenge all of these points. And the basic challenge is that all of the points are correct, but they apply only to the macroscopic world. And that world is only the most superficial layer of the larger world in which we live.

Again, let us look at Einstein's formula, $E=mc^2$. I earlier said that this formula says that matter is simply energy that has been captured into a less fluid matrix. Yet if we want to be a bit more provocative, we can say that what the formula truly says is that matter does not exist; it is a figment of our imagination. I am not hereby saying that the world we perceive with our senses is unreal and doesn't exist. I am not saying that we human beings have created the universe with our minds and can thus change it with our minds. What I am saying is that matter does not exist as we currently perceive it, and quantum physics has proven this. Let us look at each of the points listed above:

- We live in a world made of matter. Actually, we live in a world made of energy that has taken on a certain form, and we have called this form "matter."

| 1 | *Science and the Power of Self*

- Matter is "solid," meaning it has substance and continuity. Actually, matter is not solid at all. It is made from energy, and energy is a form of vibration.

- Matter is difficult to change. Actually, it is very easy to change the properties of energy waves. What we call matter is simply energy waves that are captured in a matrix. Yet they are still waves, and they are still easy to change.

- All the things we see in the macroscopic world are made from matter, and these things exist as separate units. Actually, there are no separate "things." Things appear separate only when viewed from the macroscopic perspective. From the deeper quantum perspective, everything is connected because locality is an illusion.

- Matter is separate from mind. Actually, at the quantum level there is a direct connection between matter and mind. And everything in the macroscopic world is made from quantum "stuff," meaning our minds have a potential to influence even the macroscopic world.

- Our minds have no ability to change matter directly. Actually, given that our minds can change quantum stuff and that everything is made from quantum stuff, our minds do have the ability to change matter. If we can change the quantum stuff that makes up matter, we can also change matter. We are not currently using this ability, but it still exists as our higher potential.

- The matter world has power over our minds. Actually, the matter world has no more power over our minds than what we give it through our ignorance of the quantum reality. If we look at life through the filter of the macroscopic mental box, then matter has power over our minds. But we have the potential to step outside that mental box and see the world as it really is.

The Power of Self

AN INTERCONNECTED WHOLE

With this in mind, I will sketch a new world view that can explain who we are, why we are here and what is our true potential. Let us begin by acknowledging that we do not live in a separate, isolated world. We live in a world that is one, interconnected whole. The easiest way to explain this is to say that the macroscopic world is not made from matter; it is made from energy. Energy is a form of vibration, and there are many levels of vibration. For example, we all learned in school that our eyes can detect only certain types of light.

There are forms of light that our eyes cannot detect, such as infra-red or ultra-violet as seen from Image 1:

Image 1 - The electromagnetic spectrum of light

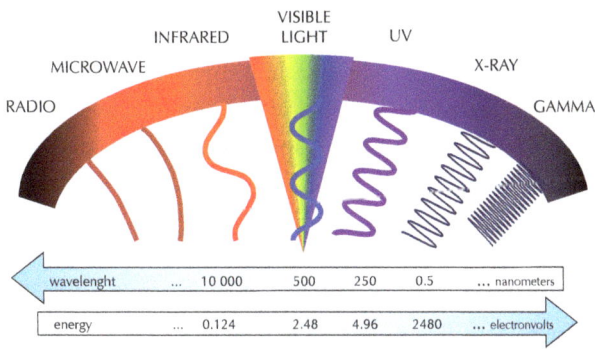

What is the difference between visible violet light and invisible ultra-violet light? The ultra-violet light has a slightly higher vibration than visible light. Other than that, there is no difference, meaning there is no impenetrable barrier that separates violet and ultra-violet light. In fact, the theory of relativity says that you can reduce the vibration of ultra-violet light and turn it into violet light. Einstein's formula even says that this is exactly how the material universe was created.

| 1 | *Science and the Power of Self*

We all learned in school that you can take a mathematical formula and divide with the same factor on both sides of the equal sign. If we do this to Einstein's formula, we get the following:

$$\frac{E}{c^2} = \frac{mc^2}{c^2}$$

We now have c^2 twice on the right side of the equal sign. Since they cancel out each other, we end up with the final formula:

$$\frac{E}{c^2} = m$$

What does this new formula tell us? It tells us that the matter world is made from a substance that is not matter, but a form of pure energy. This energy, E, vibrates at a level that is far beyond what we normally call energy, such as sunlight or electricity. It is still made from waves, but they vibrate at at level that is much higher than anything in the material world. Thus, in order to create the material world, this quantum energy had to be reduced in vibration to a certain spectrum. And this reduction factor is what Einstein said is the speed of light squared.

As you probably know, the speed of light is a very large number, and when you square it, you get an astronomical number. Which means that the original energy, E, was reduced by a huge factor in order to become material energy. Once this reduction had taken place, the material energy could now be captured into matrices that made it appear as solid and localized particles. These particles could then be used to build localized structures, such as atoms, molecules, planets, espresso machines, galaxies and human bodies.

What we now see is that we live in a world that is a continuum of vibrations.

Image 2 - A continuum of vibrations

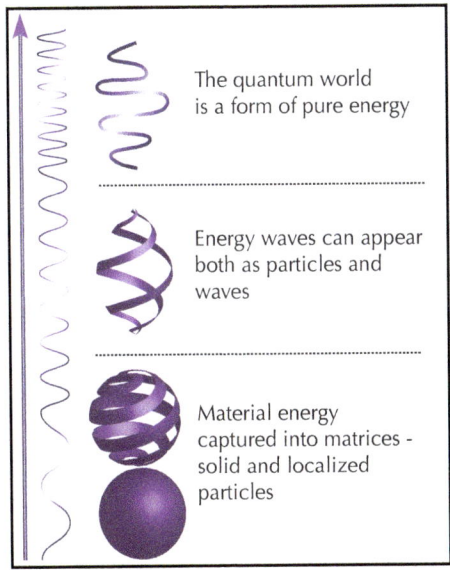

Theoretically, you could go towards higher and higher vibrations forever, but we can at least say that there are forms of vibration that are astronomically higher than anything in the material spectrum. This can explain why we cannot detect anything beyond the material world with our senses and most scientific instruments. Since we are inside the material spectrum, there is an observation horizon beyond which we cannot easily see. Yet it seems that quantum physicists have at least begun to see beyond the material spectrum. And perhaps the mind also has this ability, when developed.

HOW PURE ENERGY BECOMES MATTER

The Big Bang is normally pictured as a giant explosion, in which all of the energy and matter required to build the present universe was hurled outwards in a random, chaotic way. Based on what we have seen above, we might say that the Big Bang was truly triggered by the fact that a large amount of quantum stuff was simultaneously reduced in vibration, until it came within the material spectrum. It was this reduction of energy that started the Big Bang, and it is still what drives the expansion of the universe.

As we have seen, the quantum stuff was first reduced until it took on the form of what we call energy, meaning light, electricity, magnetism

1 | Science and the Power of Self

and so forth. These material energy waves were then captured into matrices, until they took on the form of subatomic particles. These particles were then organized into atoms, that were organized into molecules, that were used to build visible "things." What exactly causes the quantum stuff to start organizing into structures, and what determined the exact form of those structures? Why does the structured universe exist, and why does it have the form it has?

To explain the problem more clearly, consider that the Big Bang is pictured as a giant explosion. You have probably seen pictures on TV of how a building is blown up. You have probably seen this in slow-motion, and you can see how the force of the explosion is quite chaotic and seemingly random. It starts with an organized structure, but the explosion blows it apart until only disorganized bits and pieces are left. You may even have seen the film played in reverse, so that you start with the bits and pieces, and then they magically begin organizing themselves into a complete building.

When the original energy is reduced it becomes material energy that can now be captured into matrices that make it appear as solid and localized particles.

Of course, we know this backwards movie contradicts the real world. You can't blow apart an old apartment building and have the pieces spontaneously reorganize themselves into a bunch of nice villas. It simply doesn't happen this way; an explosion always produces chaos, never organized structures. Yet some people are actually claiming that the explosion of the Big Bang did – through a spontaneous, random and unconscious process – produce the incredibly complex yet orderly structure we call the universe. Who ordered that?

THE UNIVERSE AFTER THE BIG BANG

The answer is that we human beings are not the only self-aware beings in the larger world. Beyond the material spectrum, there are also self-aware beings. These beings have a creative ability, which makes it possible for them to reduce the vibration of quantum stuff to a lower spectrum. Thus, it was a group of such beings that lowered the vibration of quantum stuff to the material spectrum, and this initiated the Big Bang.

Yet even after the Big Bang, these creative beings did not simply let the universe unfold randomly. They have used their creative powers to guide the unfoldment of the universe, meaning they are the ones who have caused energy to take on certain forms and then produce very complex structures. This does not mean that the creative beings are micromanagers, who take care of every little detail. Once they had brought sufficient energy into the material spectrum, they defined certain laws that guided the unfoldment of the material world. Yet even these laws cannot fully explain the unfoldment of the universe. There have been certain critical times, when the creative beings have stepped in and have taken the evolutionary process to a new level.

One of these times was when the evolutionary process had brought forth physical bodies with a very complex brain and nervous system. At that point, the creative beings sent extensions of their own minds down to inhabit these bodies. We are those extensions, which means we have the same basic creative abilities as our "quantum parents." Only, we do not – yet – have these abilities fully developed.

This means that we were created in order to serve as co-creators with beings in a higher realm. These ascended beings have created the material world from the outside, yet we are meant to co-create it from the inside. We are meant to build upon – or tear down if we so choose – the foundation built by the creative beings.

1 | Science and the Power of Self

OUR HIGHER AND LOWER POTENTIAL

In the introduction I said we are currently trapped in a certain mental box, and it acts like a filter that prevents us from seeing the full picture of how the world really works. We will later take a closer look at the box and why we became trapped in it, but for now I want to make the point that our mental box tells us we are separate beings. We are separated from our spiritual source—if such a source even exists. We are separated from each other—which explains all human conflict. And we are separated from the material universe—which explains environmental problems.

Yet the real problem with our mental box is that it blinds us to our higher potential. As a result, we function at a very low level, and at this level we think we are trapped in and limited by the macroscopic world. And here is the key realization: in our current state of consciousness, we are indeed subject to the laws of nature that function at the macroscopic level. We have free will, which means that for all practical purposes, we are who we think we are. We currently think we are limited human beings, so that is what we are.

Yet the higher reality is that our minds have the capacity to reach beyond the macroscopic level. Our minds can indeed reach into the quantum world, and at this level they can interact with the very stuff out of which the macroscopic world is made. And when we learn to use our creative abilities to make changes at the quantum level, we can set in motion impulses that will also generate changes at the macroscopic level. Physicists have realized that quantum laws can override natural laws. For example, if you bounce a tennis ball against a wall long enough, there is a potential that a quantum tunneling effect will make it go through the wall. So far, physicists see these quantum events as extremely rare. Yet what if our higher potential is that we can deliberately produce events that override the macroscopic laws?

The Power of Self

HOW THE WORLD WAS CREATED

So here is how the world was created. The world is made from a basic kind of stuff, which I have so far called quantum stuff. This stuff is a form of energy with a very high vibration. At its highest vibration, it cannot take on form, but when you reduce its vibration, it becomes like a clay that can be shaped into distinct forms. Thus, the material world was created by taking a large quantity of quantum stuff and reducing it in vibration, until it started vibrating as what we call energy. Some of this energy was then formed into what we call subatomic particles, and out of these particles were formed more complex structures, from atoms to galaxies.

So we might say that the basic stuff out of which the world is made is a formless substance that can take on any form. Yet this substance is not able to take on form by itself. In order to take on form, the quantum stuff must be acted upon by a being with self-awareness. Why is such a creative being needed? Because only when you have self-awareness, do you have imagination and free will. Imagination empowers you to envision a form that does not yet exist. And free will allows you to choose to project your mental image upon the quantum stuff.

There are a number of creative beings who exist in a level of vibration that is beyond the material spectrum. They have the ability to reduce the vibration of quantum stuff, meaning they can bring more energy into the material spectrum. They also have the ability to form mental images and to superimpose them upon material energy, thereby creating the forms we see in the macroscopic world. It was these beings who created the macroscopic world, and they are still serving to uphold it and to guide its unfoldment.

However, once the macroscopic world had reached a certain level of complexity, the creative beings sent extensions of themselves into it. We are such extensions, and we have been given the same basic creative abilities as our quantum "parents." At present, most of us have not fully developed these creative abilities; we are not even aware of them. Nevertheless, it is still our highest potential to become fully conscious of who we are, to master our own minds and to master our ability to co-create the macroscopic world.

This means that we have two options in life. We can continue to function at our current level, which means we are subject to the laws of nature and the whole range of material limitations. At this level, the only way to change our lives is to use our physical bodies or to create technology that can change the material world.

The other option is to go through a fundamental shift in consciousness, so we become aware of who we are and unlock our true creative potential. This will empower us to use our minds to bring quantum stuff into the material world, meaning we will have a creative power that is beyond the physical body and technology. It will also empower us to use our minds to make changes directly at the quantum level, which means we can change things at the macroscopic level that we currently think are beyond change.

CHAPTER 2

HOW THE ASCENDED MASTERS CAN HELP YOU

What we have done in the previous chapter is to start out with science, which is a good example of how we human beings have taken what we can see from inside our mental box, and then we have gradually expanded our vision and understanding from there. However, what quantum physics has now done is to prove that there must be something beyond the box of the material universe. And this something must have a form of consciousness that is more sophisticated than our own. At this point, this is as far as science can take us; this is as far as we can go by looking from inside the box.

So let us now take this and ask a logical question: If there are beings outside the material universe, if these beings have created the universe and if they have sent us in here to co-create the world with them, is it likely that they would just leave us alone? And if they haven't left us alone, is it possible that they have given us teachings that can tell us something that we simply could not see from inside the box? And could these teachings help us unlock the power of Self and ultimately ascend permanently beyond the human mental box and the material universe? In other words, there will come a point on your personal path, where you need to consider what kind of teacher you want: one who is inside the human mental box or one who is outside of it?

| 2 | *How the ascended masters can help you*

WHAT KIND OF TEACHER DO YOU WANT?

As we have seen, you are right now looking at life through a particular sense of self. We might say that this self forms a mental box around the real you, and the mental box colors they way you see everything, including yourself. So the very key to changing your Life Experience is to go beyond the mental box, to see something that is outside the limitations that seem so real. Yet you simply cannot do that by using the ideas, beliefs, experiences and perceptions that are already inside the box.

Why not? Because everything you see from inside the box will only confirm the reality of the box. The only way to break the spell is to reach for something that will challenge the box, some frame of reference that is beyond the box. So where do you get it? Well, the simple answer is that you need a teacher who is not inside your personal mental box. Let me illustrate this with an example.

As a child you probably worked on some of these little puzzles, where you have to draw a line through a labyrinth in order to find a treasure in the middle. Here is a simple example:

Image 3 - Maze

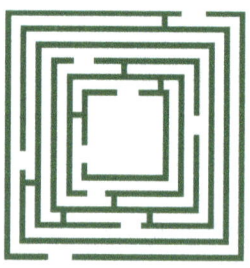

You may even have visited a real labyrinth or maze made out of tall hedges that form a complex pattern. Once you are inside such a labyrinth, you have a very limited perspective. All you can see is green walls that form a narrow corridor. As you walk down the corridor, you run into a wall, but to one side is an opening. If you turn, you end up in another corridor, which leads to another one. Once in a while you come to a place where there are two or more openings. You choose one, but it only leads to a dead end,

The Power of Self

and now you have to retrace your steps in order to get back to where you started. You can then choose another opening, hoping it will lead you somewhere.

Isn't this a fitting metaphor for how we all start out in life? We have a very limited perspective on life, and all we can see is our immediate environment. We have no clear idea of how we got into this mess and where it is all leading—if anywhere. And the real problem is that while we are inside the labyrinth, we don't have a map, so how can we know where we are and how to get to the exit?

Now imagine that as you are fumbling around, you meet a person who tells you she has found this wonderful open space in the labyrinth, where there is a fountain with refreshing waters. She gives you directions, and after some twists and turns, you manage to find the place. It is nice to be in an open space and the water is great, but after a while, you realize you are still stuck in the maze and you still have no idea where the exit is—or whether there even is an exit.

The person you met is a symbol for people who have found something you haven't found, and thus they can indeed give you valid advice. Yet they are still as stuck in the maze as you are. So now imagine that you come to the realization, that you have had enough of walking around blindly. You want something different. You want advice from someone who has cracked the code and found the way out of the maze. You want directions from someone who has found a map and can help you plot a course to the exit.

You then find an opening with a bench, so you sit down and lean back. Suddenly, you look up, and you see a tall tower rising out of the maze. It has a round platform on top, and around it are a number of figures who are giving directions to people down in the maze. You realize that these figures can see the maze from above, so they can tell exactly where you are relative to the exit. You then jump up on the bench and start waving your arms in order to get the attention of one of the figures in the tower. One of them soon notices you and asks what you want. You tell him you want to get out, and he tells you: "Start walking!"

As you begin to follow the directions of your elevated guide, you realize he has a unique way of teaching. He won't make choices for you, but he will give you enough of a hint that you can figure it out for yourself. In fact, after a while, you begin to realize that while he is taking you towards the exit, he is not taking you along the most direct route. The reason is that your guide realizes there are certain experiences you need to have before you are ready to leave the maze behind. And he skillfully guides you to exactly where you need to go in order to take the next step.

OUR UNIVERSAL TEACHERS

This book will outline a systematic path that can help you develop your own personal relationship with our spiritual or ascended teachers and with your own higher self. The elevated guides in the tower of my fictional maze are a symbol for these teachers. They have been in embodiment as we are, so they know what we are going through. Yet they have solved the human enigma and found their way out of the maze, so they can give us a perspective that we could not get from inside the labyrinth.

We all have one of these teachers assigned to us, and they have been guiding us on our personal journey to the extent that we have been able to hear them and willing to follow their directions. The purpose of this book is to make you consciously aware of your spiritual teachers, so you can start following their directions in a more awakened and deliberate way—which will naturally speed up your progress tremendously.

If you apply the teachings and tools in this book, you will soon stop feeling like you are bumbling around in a hostile environment and getting nowhere. Instead, you will come to feel that you are – and always have been – following exactly the path that you personally need to follow in order to get where you really want to go in life. This includes finding the places you need to visit inside the maze while moving ever closer to the exit—which is really the entry to a much broader level of reality.

YOU ARE READY FOR A HIGHER TEACHING

As I already mentioned, the basic credo of our spiritual teachers is this: "When the student is ready, the teacher appears." You have found this book, which means that at some level of your being, you are ready for the teachings and tools offered by our ascended teachers. Yet think back to the metaphor of the maze. The reality is that each of us has a personal maze that we need to navigate in order to find our way in life. And that maze exists inside our own minds.

The key to increasing your awareness of Self is to cultivate the habit of self-observation.

Your personal maze is made up of the beliefs and experiences you have had on your total journey in the material universe. The point being that while you are certainly ready for this book at the deeper levels of your being, it is entirely possible that you have certain hurdles you need to overcome before you can make full use of this book. You may have certain beliefs or preconceived opinions that block your acceptance of what this book teaches. Or they might block you from applying the tools you will receive.

The way to deal with this is to realize a simple truth. The essential key to unlocking the power of Self is to become more aware of the Self. And the key to increasing your awareness of Self is to cultivate the habit of self-observation. Let me put this another way. Unlocking the power of Self is a matter of finding your way to the center – the treasure chamber – of your personal maze. Yet your maze is very tricky, because there is no pathway that leads directly to the center. Just take a closer look at the maze on Image 3 (see the next page).

The walls in your maze are made out of your limiting beliefs and preconceived opinions—they are like the hedge plants in a real labyrinth.

| 2 | *How the ascended masters can help you*

Image 3 - Maze

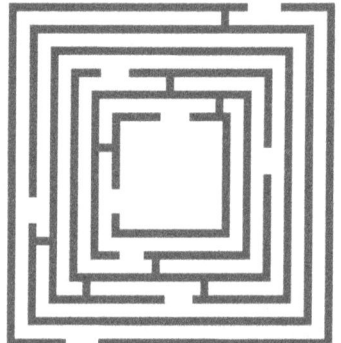

So it is not a matter of finding an open pathway, because there is none. All of the pathways are blocked by your pet opinions.

How do you crack the enigma; how do you get to the center of Self? Well, when you come to a dead end, you have to take a different approach. The dead end is blocked by an opinion or belief that you have never actually taken a look at, because you have always taken it for granted. So what you have to do is to step back and take a critical look. You have to question why you believe what you believe, and you have to see how it limits your progress. And then you have to decide to walk right through it, in order to find the pathway that is hidden behind the unexamined belief.

The dead end of your personal growth is an opinion or belief that you have never actually taken a look at, because you have always taken it for granted.

Imagine that you are in a real maze, and after walking around for a long time, you realize there simply is no pathway that leads to the center. Yet when taking a critical look, you realize that the plants that form the hedges have narrow openings between them. So instead of walking around the walls, you have to take a fundamentally different approach and walk *through* the walls. And only then will you make progress towards your personal treasure chamber.

The Power of Self

WHAT IS AN ASCENDED MASTER?

As we have seen, the material world is made out of the same stuff as the spiritual world, only the energy has been reduced to a lower vibration than the spiritual realm. This means that the spiritual realm is not separated from our world by some kind of barrier. The material world exists within the larger energy field of the spiritual realm. The spiritual world is right around us; only it has a higher vibration so we cannot see it. Yet we can sense it through our intuitive faculties, as we will see later.

Image 4 - The Spiritual World is around us

We have also seen that our consciousness can interact with quantum stuff, and the reason is that there is a form of consciousness at the quantum level. That consciousness is a number of self-aware beings who have created the material world. These beings could be called creative beings, quantum beings or our ascended or spiritual teachers. Yet I prefer to call them the ascended masters. The term "ascended master" indicates something important. An ascended being was once in a denser realm, as we are now, and has then ascended from there. The ascended master qualified for this ascension by attaining mastery over its own mind, thereby unlocking its creative potential and attaining mastery over its environment. It was this mastery that qualified it for the ascension and made it an ascended master. Take note that not all ascended masters ascended from earth, but they did ascend from a situation similar to what we face.

The process followed by all ascended masters is the exact same process that we are engaged in right now. We are all ascended masters in the making. This means that the ascended masters know from first-hand

| 2 | *How the ascended masters can help you*

experience what we are going through. They started out with a limited state of consciousness, just as we have right now. They then gradually climbed towards greater mastery, until they attained the full mastery that is our own very realistic potential. This means the ascended masters are the perfect teachers for us. They are not some high-and-mighty god-like figures, who are sitting up there on a pink cloud without ever getting their hands dirty. They know exactly what it feels like to be trapped at the macroscopic level, but they also know how to systematically climb towards the mastery of mind over matter.

The ascended masters do not have a physical body like we do, and as a result they do not perceive the world through the limited senses of the body. This means they see far more than we see; they have a much more complete view of the world and how it works. Which is another reason they can be useful to us as seekers of higher understanding.

WHY HAVE YOU NEVER HEARD ABOUT ASCENDED MASTERS?

Why have you never been told that we have ascended teachers? Well, partly because the term has only been in use for a little over a century, but you have actually heard about the influence of universal spiritual teachers throughout history.

Our spiritual teachers have only one goal, namely to help us raise our state of consciousness. They do not – repeat: do not – seek to accomplish this goal by developing the ultimate religion or thought system. Instead, they work with people at whatever level they are at, and they seek to help them rise to the next level up. The ascended masters work with a civilization based on its current world view, and then they seek to help people by introducing ideas that people can accept but which can help them transcend their current world view. Thus, the masters often work incognito by inspiring people in embodiment, and people have no idea where their brilliant ideas come from.

There have always been universal teachers offering their assistance to people who are open. Throughout the ages, they have sought to work with many different individuals in order to introduce new ideas, that could help people in a given culture and at a given level of consciousness come up higher. The ascended masters have inspired all of the world's major religions and many lesser-known religions. They have inspired many philosophical ideas. They have inspired literature, music, plays and other cultural phenomena. They have inspired science and many forms of technology, because this has given us the freedom to pursue personal growth, rather than working at the "sweat of our brow."

Yet the masters also attempt to give people who are open a more coherent collection of universal ideas, and these ideas will be presented in this book. You can then make your own evaluation of whether they can help you answer life's fundamental questions.

WHY IS THERE NO PROOF THAT THE MASTERS EXIST?

If the ascended masters have been with us throughout human history, why isn't their existence commonly accepted? The most basic reason is that planet earth is subject to the Law of Free Will. This means that plausible deniability must be maintained, and that is why the masters cannot give us an irrefutable proof of their existence.

The ascended masters teach that there are numerous planets in the universe that are inhabited by self-aware beings like us. A planet is a kind of schoolroom for the inhabitants, so one can evaluate a planet based on how far the inhabitants have developed their creative abilities. Is the collective consciousness at the kindergarten level or have the inhabitants risen to the college level?

Planet earth is currently at a rather low level of development, which means that most inhabitants on earth are below a certain level of awareness. This is the level where people have a desire to feel that they are separate beings who live in a separate world. The only way we can have that experience is because matter on earth is so dense, that it hides the fact that it is created from a finer substance. In other words, when seen through our physical senses, matter appears to be solid and appears to be existing on its own. It does not appear to be made of spiritual energy, and that is why we can believe that the material world is either separated from God or is self-contained.

The earth is currently in a transition phase, where we are rising to a higher level of collective awareness. Yet at this point, the Law of Free Will mandates that people must be able to deny the existence of God or ascended masters. People must be able to maintain the illusion that they are separate beings living in a separate world. Thus, there will not be an irrefutable proof of the existence of God or ascended masters for the foreseeable future. Which means that you can prove the existence of ascended masters only on an individual level, as we will talk about in a coming chapter.

This also explains how the teachings in this book are brought forth. Because of the need for deniability, the masters cannot let their teachings fall from the sky. Thus, they give their teachings through people who have raised their consciousness to the point, where they can make direct contact with the masters and thus receive ideas or even spoken messages from the masters. This makes it easy for people to write off the masters and their teachings by labeling them according to their present belief system.

We can now see another reason why you have never heard of ascended masters. When the student is ready, the ascended teacher appears. You cannot truly acknowledge the existence of the masters until you are ready for their teachings. Which means that since you are reading this book, you are definitely ready to take a closer look at the ascended masters and what they teach.

WHY ARE THE MASTERS IMPORTANT?

Why is it important to be open to the existence of ascended masters? The most immediate reason is that there are some answers that we simply cannot get through materialistic means or even through a certain level of consciousness. If you want answers beyond your current level of consciousness, you have to first seek these answers from a source that is

The Power of Self

beyond your level. And then, you can gradually raise your consciousness to the level, where you can validate the ideas directly from within the Self.

Consider a fact that has been largely overlooked by modern civilization, namely that the human mind can become a closed system. Look at medieval times, when the church had created a doctrine which said that the earth was the center of the universe. On top of that, the church said that if you questioned or looked beyond doctrine, you would burn forever in hell. As long as you accepted the church's claim, there was no way you could question the medieval world view.

We have all been brought up to believe that it was science that broke the church's stranglehold on the human mind, but is that the whole truth? What if the deeper reality was that some of the first scientists – who saw themselves as deeply spiritual people – were able to attune their minds to the ascended masters? And through that attunement, these early explorers were able to receive inspiration and insights for how they could take humankind to the next evolutionary level.

The ascended masters say that the growth in human knowledge has not happened only through the mind's ability to gather knowledge horizontally. It has also happened through the Self's ability to gather knowledge vertically, namely by tuning in to a higher source. That higher source is the ascended masters.

As I said, many ascended masters have been in embodiment on earth, and therefore they have an intimate understanding of the challenges we face while we look at the world through the filter of our current mental boxes. And that is precisely why they have made it their labor of love to help us transcend our limited perception, so we can not only know the Self but unleash the inherent power of the Self. Why are they doing this? Well, let us take a closer look.

WHY DO ASCENDED MASTERS CARE ABOUT US?

If ascended masters exist in a higher realm that is beyond the limitations of the material world, why would they care about us? If the spiritual realm is so much better than this world, why don't they simply enjoy themselves and leave us to fend for ourselves? Do they need anything from us; do they have some kind of agenda?

The masters teach that the consciousness through which most of us see the world is a consciousness of separation. Because we have become focused on the surface level of appearances, we are focused on the differences that set things apart. As a result, we perceive ourselves as being separated from God and the spiritual realm, we perceive ourselves as being separated from other humans, and we perceive ourselves as being separated from our environment, meaning the planet upon which we live. We are blinded by a veil of illusion, namely the illusion of separation.

Most of us see the world through the consciousness of separation, because we have become focused on the surface level of appearances.

In contrast to our view, the ascended masters are not blinded by the veil of separation. They clearly see the world the way we should see it based on the theory of relativity and quantum physics. The masters see that while there are certain divisions in the world, there are no impenetrable barriers.

Everything is made from one basic substance that has simply taken on different forms. The masters actually say that everything in both the spiritual realm and the material realm is made from a basic substance, which they call the Ma-ter light or the Mother light. This substance has no form in itself, which is why it cannot be detected by any material instruments. However, it has the potential to take on any form and we will later discuss how the Mother light takes on form.

The ascended masters see that separation is an illusion that seems plausible only when you look at the world through the filter of a certain state of consciousness. This dualistic consciousness filters out the underlying reality that everything is made from the same substance and ultimately springs from the same source.

The ascended masters do not see themselves as separated from us. The masters see themselves as extensions of beings at even higher levels, and they see that this "chain of being" goes all the way to the Creator. The masters also see that we are the latest extensions of the chain of being, and thus they see us as their own brothers and sisters. They see that we are simply trapped behind the veil of duality, also called the energy veil (abbreviated to evil). The masters clearly see that it is the illusion of separation that causes all of the conflicts and suffering found on earth, and thus they have no other desire or agenda than to offer us the tools to raise our consciousness, so we can see beyond the veil and know who we truly are.

THE PURPOSE OF THE WORLD OF FORM

The masters teach that the purpose of the world of form is to serve as an environment in which self-aware beings can start out with a very localized self-awareness, and they can then gradually expand that self-awareness. The masters teach that God is not a Being who is fundamentally different from us. The Creator is a Being with the ultimate level of self-awareness, but because we were created from the Creator's Being, we have the potential to expand our self-awareness to the same level as our Creator.

The ascended masters do not see us as being different from or lower than themselves. They see us as beings who have not yet attained their level of self-awareness, and they have volunteered to take on the role of serving as our guides or teachers. Their overall goal is to help us raise our self-awareness, but their specific goal is to help us raise our self-awareness to the point, where we are completely free from the illusion of separation.

When we do escape this illusion, we see that all life is one, and this is when we have passed the final exam in "Schoolroom Terra," which means we can now permanently move on to higher realms of energy. This is what the masters call the process of the ascension. Yet although

Christianity also talks about Jesus ascending, there are some important differences between Christian beliefs and ascended master teachings. Christianity teaches that Jesus was the only one who ascended, as even his mother was only "assumed" into heaven. Christianity also portrays this as a physical process of Jesus' body being raised to heaven.

The ascended masters teach that we all have the potential to ascend. But this is not a physical process; it is a process whereby we raise our consciousness, until we leave the physical body behind and move into a higher level of self-awareness, in which we have no need for a physical body. Instead, we take on a spiritual body, meaning a body made from the higher energy frequencies that make up the spiritual realm. And because the ascended masters have faced the same challenges we now face, they know exactly how to help us overcome these challenges and attain self-mastery.

ASCENDED MASTERS AND THE POWER OF SELF

What we have seen up until this point is that the entire material universe is made from spiritual energy that is reduced to the material frequency spectrum. This stream of energy is literally the driving force that created and sustains the universe. So when many self-help or spiritual teachings say, that by changing your mind you can change your material circumstances, what is the deeper reality behind this claim?

Consider the fact that everything at the macroscopic level is made from energy. How can you change a material circumstance, such as a disease in your body? Well, the best way to create change is to work at the level of energy, the level of cause rather than the level of effect. Why is your body sick? Because your cells have taken on so much low-frequency energy that they cannot function normally. What is the logical way to heal your body? It is to free your cells from the burden of this energy, whereby they will again function in a natural way.

Scientists have shown that when two energy waves meet, they create an interference pattern. A high-frequency wave can raise the vibration of a low-frequency wave. Consider that Jesus performed seemingly miraculous feats of healing the sick. Is it possible that these were not miracles, but a consequence of the fact that Jesus had learned to use the full creative abilities of the mind? Is it possible Jesus did this in order to show us the potential we all have?

Again, everything in the material universe is created from energy waves that have been lowered to a certain level of vibration. How can you transform these material conditions? By raising the vibration of the energy waves out of which the conditions are made. This is not some high-flung theory. It is solid science that has simply been related to self-help.

As we have seen, quantum physics has proven that there is a realm beyond the material and that our minds can interact with it. The deeper reality is that we are designed to be co-creators with the intelligent beings who created the material world. How do we co-create? Well, one aspect is that our minds are designed with the capacity to be open doors for higher spiritual energies to be lowered into the material spectrum. Right now our minds have become closed doors because something is blocking the natural flow of creative energy. The key to unlocking the power of Self is to restore this creative flow.

We co-create by being open doors for higher spiritual energies to be lowered into the material spectrum.

Yet take note of where the creative flow comes from. The ascended masters teach that the creative flow originates with the Creator. The very high energy of the Creator is then stepped down in vibration through many levels of the spiritual world. Who is stepping the creative energy down? The ascended masters who form a chain of being from the Creator to our level. When we unlock the power of Self, we can fulfill our rightful role as the latest link in the chain of being, we can find our place in the creative flow, what the masters call the River of Life.

Yet when we do find this place, from where will we get our creative energy? We will get it from the link in the chain of being that is right above us. And that link is the ascended masters who work most closely with earth. So the final conclusion to this chapter is that we need to know about ascended masters because the very key to unlocking the power of Self is that we learn to work with the masters right above us. Unless we can receive light directly from the masters, we cannot unlock the full creative powers of the Self.

TWO WAYS TO CHANGE OUR LIVES

When we consider how we can change our material circumstances, we have two basic options. Our first option is that we can seek to use the energy that is already in the material spectrum. This is indeed what many self-help and even some religious and spiritual philosophies teach. However, there are three problems with this approach:

- There is only a finite amount of energy in the material spectrum. Thus, from the outset, there is a limit to our creative powers.

- This energy has already been reduced to a certain level, which means its creative power is limited. You cannot solve a problem created with material energy by using another form of material energy. You need a higher form of energy to truly change a material condition.

- There are seven billion other people on earth who are fighting for their share of a finite amount of material energy. So if you seek to change your life by using material energy, you will have to take that energy from someone else. And that means you will lock yourself in a perpetual struggle against other people, as we can see going on throughout human history.

The Power of Self

Our second option is to realize that our minds are designed to receive creative energy from a higher realm. And when we make use of this ability, our creative power is far beyond what can be achieved through material energy. The way to receive this energy is to work with the beings in that higher realm, namely the ascended masters. Yet before we consider how this works, let us look at how you can know that the masters really do exist. This will also show us something important about how you can learn to work with the masters on an individual basis.

CHAPTER 3

ARE THE ASCENDED MASTERS REAL?

How can you know that the ascended masters really exist? If you look at history, there are generally two ways for people to resolve the question of what is real and unreal. One is the approach taken by mainstream religion, where you claim some absolute authority that people should not question. The other way is the one taken by materialistic science, where it is claimed that only what can be studied and measured with scientific instruments has any reality.

When it comes to proving the existence of ascended masters, neither of these methods will work. The masters make no claim to authority based on a tradition or organization in this world. In fact, they refuse to let themselves be limited by any earthly authority or organization. Nor can their existence be proven by scientific methods (at least not at this time). So where does that leave you—is there anything beyond these two methods? Indeed, there is, and it is your ability to gain knowledge from within the Self.

This is what has traditionally been called a mystical or intuitive approach. Historically speaking, a mystical approach is the alternative to the authority of religion and the materialistic proof of science. Most mainstream religions have a mystical branch; in fact the founders of those religions were usually mystics.

You might wonder why you have never heard much about mysticism, and the reason is twofold. Firstly, neither mainstream religion nor materialistic science recognizes mysticism. Secondly, mysticism doesn't really advertise itself, as mystics know people have to come to a certain level of spiritual maturity before they are ready for the mystical approach.

The key to true objectivity is to understand the nature of the mind.

What is the mystical approach? In its essence, the mystical approach says that there is a way to know reality that is beyond any authority in this world, including materialistic proof. That way is an inner way, namely to have an intuitive, mystical experience. You do not believe what a religious or political authority tells you and you do not believe what a scientific authority tells you. You accept only what you have had confirmed through a direct, inner experience.

Obviously, the authority figures in this world will say this is an entirely subjective experience, but that is because they do not understand the nature of a mystical experience (which means they have never had a powerful mystical experience). While it is certainly true that many human beliefs are highly subjective, this is not the complete picture, and science itself has delivered the best proof of this. The development of quantum physics has invalidated the materialist position that we can attain objectivity by shutting out the mind. Instead, quantum physics has proven that the key to true objectivity is to understand the nature of the mind—which is exactly what mystics have been seeking for thousands of years.

A MYSTICAL APPROACH TO OBJECTIVITY

What do the ascended masters, and mysticism in general, have to say about the objectivity problem? For thousands of years, mystics have been saying that the human mind has the capacity to be in two distinctly different states of consciousness. In one state, everything we see is colored by a filter, meaning our experience of the world is entirely subjective. Yet in the other state, we have attained clear or neutral vision, so we see things the way they are, meaning we have a truly objective view of the world.

Of course, there is a third stage, in which we have started having glimpses of the objective state of mind, but our vision is still – to a larger or smaller degree – colored by the subjective state. Which means that it is possible for two people to have genuine mystical experiences and interpret them to mean different things. For example, a Christian and a Muslim can both be convinced that a mystical experience confirmed the validity of their religion.

The path outlined by the ascended masters is a process, where we start out with a glimpse of a higher state of consciousness. And then we gradually purify our minds from all subjective elements, until we obtain pure vision. This higher state can be called many names, such as enlightenment, naked awareness or Christ consciousness. The teachings of the ascended masters are designed to help us complete this journey towards a higher state of consciousness.

You will not truly recognize the existence of the masters until you have a mystical experience.

In today's age, the masters' teachings are freely available in books and on websites that anyone can find. Thus, it is possible that people can find the teachings without having had an intuitive experience. People might recognize the value of the teachings based on intellectual reasoning, because the teachings can indeed answer many questions. Yet in order to truly resolve the question of whether the masters are real, you need to have an inner experience. This experience will not give you what we normally call proof; it will give you a subtle sense of "inner knowing," whereby you recognize something as obviously real.

Having said this, we also have to recognize a very real concern about personal experiences. You can indeed find many people – including many spiritual seekers – who believe in the most improbable things. For example, every year some of the people who visit Jerusalem and follow in Jesus' footsteps, become convinced that they are Christ come again and that it is up to them to save the world. When you understand mystical experiences, you realize that they must be approached in a very specific way.

THE KALEIDOSCOPE OF THE MIND

The ascended masters have some profound teachings about intuition. They compare the human mind to a kaleidoscope. You will know that a kaleidoscope is a tube, and inside of it are several dividers, in between which are sandwiched colored glass pieces. When you rotate the tube, the glass pieces are rearranged and form various color patterns.

The glass pieces compare to the many ideas and beliefs that we have in our conscious and subconscious minds. When we encounter a certain situation in life, the kaleidoscope of the mind is rotated in a way that creates a specific color pattern—which then becomes our conscious experience of the situation. One profound implication of this is that our experience of life – our Life Experience – is determined by the ideas we have in our minds and how they are arranged by specific situations.

The masters teach that most people go through life in an unaware way. A given situation triggers a certain reactionary pattern, and people's choices are entirely colored by the glass pieces in the kaleidoscope of their minds. They react without being aware of why they react as they do, often thinking this is the only way for them to react to a certain type of situation. Such people do not have control over their reactions, because they have not taken a look at the contents of the conscious and subconscious minds. They have not been willing to look at the beam in their own eyes.

In contrast to this, the masters offer a path of self-mastery, whereby we can gradually attain control over our reactions to the situations we

| 3 | *Are the ascended masters real?*

encounter in the material world. We can learn to make free and objective choices, instead of having our reactions determined by old patterns in the subconscious mind. Yet this path begins with one fundamental realization.

The masters offer a path of self-mastery, whereby we can gradually attain control over our reactions to the situations we encounter.

When you look through a kaleidoscope, it is easy to focus on the intricate color patterns, and this is indeed what most people do. When we think about our minds, we often focus on the thoughts that fill our minds. Most people simply don't see anything beyond the contents of their own minds. Yet now ask yourself a simple question: "Why is it possible for me to see the colored patterns in a kaleidoscope?" The explanation is that there is light entering the other end of the kaleidoscope, and this light – in contrast to the colored patterns – is *not* produced by the kaleidoscope. This simple realization becomes very profound when transferred to the mind.

What mystics have always been saying is that the very fact that we are conscious, that we have self-awareness, proves that there must be a stream of spiritual energy and consciousness, that enters our minds from a higher source. As we have seen, this is perfectly in line with quantum physics. Given that our minds can interact with the level of subatomic particles, it is obvious that our minds can serve as vehicles, chalices, for a stream of higher, spiritual energy.

Most people are unaware of this energy, as they are focused on the contents of consciousness instead of consciousness itself. They see only the color patterns in the kaleidoscope, without considering the light that creates them. When you have a mystical experience, it is because you spontaneously focus on the light behind the color patterns. You experience awareness in a more pure form.

However, here is the important point. All people are capable of having a mystical experience, and many people have indeed had such experiences. Yet being aware that the colored patterns in the mind are created by light from a higher source is not the same as having a pure vision of that light.

It is very important to realize, that there must be a form of awareness beyond the colored patterns of everyday thoughts, yet this is only the first step in a gradual process. Because as long as you are seeing the light through your existing beliefs and ideas, the light is still colored by the contents of your mind. Meaning that you still don't see reality as it really is.

THE ESSENCE OF MYSTICISM

The path of the mystic is a process, whereby we gradually cleanse the mind from all of the limited ideas, beliefs, paradigms and assumptions that spring from the material world. In other words, we gradually throw out some of the colored glass pieces, and one day we will see the light entering the mind without having it colored at all. This is what we might call a pure mystical experience, an experience of pure awareness. Yet there might still be some limited beliefs left in our minds, and the true mystic will continue the cleansing process until the mind is free from all limiting ideas.

Why is this important? The ascended masters say that you will not truly recognize the existence of the masters until you have a mystical experience. Before that, you might recognize the masters intellectually and understand the value of their teachings in a purely intellectual way. Yet only when we have the direct inner experience, will we truly see that the masters are real, and only then will we begin to fully appreciate what their teachings can do for us and the world.

The all-important point is that when we have our first mystical experience, our minds will still have many glass pieces. Thus, the experience

| 3 | Are the ascended masters real?

itself can be colored by the beliefs we hold, which raises the danger that a mystical experience can be interpreted as an absolute confirmation of the validity of certain beliefs.

A true mystic recognizes that a mystical experience is indeed valid. However, the validity of it is *not* that it proves a particular belief. The validity of the mystical experience is that it proves there is a state of consciousness that is beyond *all* beliefs found on earth. The validity of the mystical experience is that it proves there is a source of light outside the narrow tube of the kaleidoscope. And the mystic then makes it a priority to experience that light without any filter.

WHY IS THE MYSTICAL APPROACH SO IMPORTANT?

The ascended masters are the true mystic of the ages. Before they ascended, they continued to question all of their cherished beliefs, until they started having more and more pure mystical experiences. Instead of using these transcendental experiences as proof for an earthly belief system, they took the experiences as proof that there is a need to always look beyond the outer form, constantly seeking for the pure, uncolored experience of the spiritual light. They saw the light as a lifeline to their source, and they kept following the lifeline, until they did indeed unite with their source in the ritual of the ascension.

The masters have only one basic message: "What one has done, all can do." They have proven that we can transcend all human limitations, and they want us to know that we can do the same. But in order to do so, we need to follow the time-tested process of continuing to transcend all limited beliefs, until we attain the pure state of awareness that allows us to experience reality as it is, with no filter and no sense of distance or separation.

Why is this important? Because the reality is that spiritual light wants to flow into this world. The ascended masters know that the key to truly transforming the earth is to let more light flow into this world, because when people begin to see more clearly, they will naturally make better choices. The masters are constantly ready to pour light into this world, so why don't they just flood the world with light until no darkness is left?

The answer is the Law of Free Will, which says that the inhabitants of the earth must be allowed to have the experience they want. Right now, most people on earth have chosen to have an experience of being separated from God. This experience is possible only because the world is not flooded with spiritual light. So how can more light come into the material frequency spectrum? The light can come only through the minds of people in embodiment—people like you and me. We have a right to choose to bring in light through our minds, even if the majority want to live in darkness.

The real key to unlocking the power of self is not to find a magical formula that forces the light. The key is to empty your mind of the elements that block the flow of light.

Yet what will it take for our minds to become open doors for spiritual light? The light comes from the ascended masters, who represent the level above us in the chain of being. So the only way for us to receive light from the masters is for us to attune our minds to the masters. And ultimately this means we must follow the mystical path of seeking oneness with the level of reality that is right above ours. We all have the potential to attune our minds to the mind of an ascended master, and even to ultimately attain a sense of oneness with that master. This is the path that the beings who are now ascended have followed before us, and we are fully capable of going through that same process.

Yet this process of attunement leading to oneness must take place inside your minds. Do you begin to see why this is important? There are self-help or spiritual books who will tell you that you need some kind of secret formula in order to get the power to change your life. Yet the deeper reality is that the true power of Self is the flow of spiritual light through your mind. This is a completely natural process. The light wants to flow, and it will inevitably flow through any opening in the veil that "separates" the spiritual and the material realm.

So the real key to unlocking the power of self is *not* to find some kind of magical formula that forces the light. The key is to empty your mind of the elements that block the flow of light. As your mind is purified, the light will spontaneously and naturally flow. Yet your personal blocks are all inside your mind, and that is why they can only be resolved there. And they can only be resolved through conscious choices, where you see why certain beliefs limit you and then decide to accept a higher reality that comes from a mystical vision.

The ascended masters face a delicate task. They can give us outer teachings, but the outer teaching itself will not change you. The only value of the outer teaching is that you can use it as a catalyst for having a mystical, intuitive experience. And when you do have such an experience, then your consciousness will shift. This leads to the question of how to clear your mind, and we will look at this in one of the coming chapters. But first we will sketch the cosmological world view presented by the ascended masters. It is very helpful to have the big picture before you get too caught up in the details.

CHAPTER 4

HOW THE WORLD OF FORM WAS CREATED

In this chapter we will look at the basic cosmology of the ascended masters, meaning how and why the universe was created and the basic laws according to which it functions. I know this might seem theoretical and abstract to some readers, but it will set a foundation that will help us explain the true nature of the self and its potential to be an open door for a higher power. It will also help us better understand the practical path that will be outlined in the following section.

THE HIERARCHICAL STRUCTURE OF THE UNIVERSE

Science has shown us that the universe has a hierarchical structure. Everything at the macroscopic level is made from molecules, and thus it can be created only within the framework set by the laws that guide the function of molecules. However, molecules are made from atoms, and are thus subject to the laws that guide the working of atoms—and so on towards deeper levels. The ascended masters agree with the hierarchical structure discovered by science, but they extend it much further, ultimately leading to the Creator, who forms the top of the hierarchical pyramid.

However, the Creator described by the ascended masters is very different from the traditional image of God. It is especially different from the monotheistic image of an all-male God, sitting on a great white

| 4 | *How the world of form was created*

throne and judging human beings, sending some to eternal torment in hell.

The ascended masters make a distinction between the world in which we live and what is beyond that world. They say that our world is the "world of form," because everything in it has a form that sets it apart from other forms. This is what makes it possible for us to start out with a limited self-awareness and then grow towards higher levels of self-awareness. It even makes it possible for us to believe we are separate beings, meaning we are separated from God, from the matter world and from each other.

Yet even this can become a source of our growth in self-awareness. The reason is that we grow in self-awareness by consciously recognizing that we are in a limited state, that we are more than that state, and then making a conscious choice to rise to a higher state. Thus, no matter how limited our present state might be, it can still be a foundation for our growth.

WHAT IS BEYOND THE WORLD OF FORM

One of the fundamental problems for the ascended masters is that we humans are so used to seeing life based on the world of form – specifically the material universe – and we are so used to communicating with words. Words are clearly developed based on a world of separate forms, and they are best suited to describing forms that are clearly set apart from others. As our senses are designed to work with contrast, so are words best suited for describing clearly defined or linear differentiation.

It is difficult to use words to describe the part of reality that is beyond our world of form. Consequently, the masters have said little about it, but they have given it a name: the "Allness." The linear mind immediately wants to ask where this world came from, when it was created, who created it and why. Yet these are questions that have meaning only in a world of differentiated forms, for only in such a world can one create a linear timeline. The Allness has always existed and thus has no beginning or end. It is a non-linear world, and thus very difficult to comprehend for beings in a linear world.

Image 5 - Non-linear void

What is important to know is that in the Allness there can be no separate forms. Thus, in the Allness it is not possible to do what we are doing now, namely start out with a limited sense of awareness and then grow towards a broader state of consciousness. Thus, the being who created our world of form chose to create our world as a way for itself to grow and as a way for us to grow. In order to do this, our Creator had to first create a sphere with slightly different characteristics than the Allness.

HOW OUR WORLD WAS CREATED

Each particular world of form is created by an individual being, who has the level of consciousness of a Creator. A Creator starts the process of creating a world of form by setting itself apart from the Allness. Since we have to use linear words and concepts, we might say that the Creator defines a spherical boundary around itself. It creates a sphere that exists inside the Allness, but does not have the same level of vibration as the Allness. It is set apart from the whole.

4 | How the world of form was created

Image 6 - Singularity

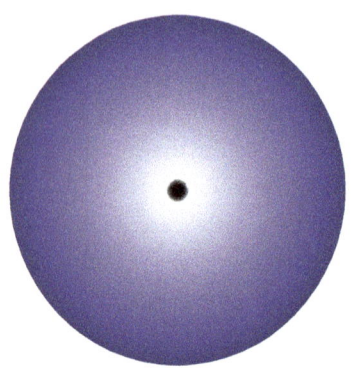

As the next step, the Creator withdraws itself from the space inside this boundary. The Creator withdraws itself into a singularity, and the rest of the sphere becomes a void. Again, in linear words we might say that the Allness is filled with a very high form of energy, which makes it impossible to create divisions or to create the impression that something is separated from the Allness. In order to create a world with seemingly separate forms, the Creator first has to create a void that has no energy and no forms. It is void.

As the next step, the Creator creates the basic energy that will be used to construct the world of form. The masters call this the Ma-ter light or the Mother light. The reason for calling it a name that sounds feminine is that in order to create a world with separate forms, the Creator must define two separate forces or elements.

For anything to be created, there must be an outgoing or expansive force. This is what the Creator uses to project something out from the singularity in the center of the void. Yet if this outgoing force was not balanced with a contracting force, no form could be created or sustained.

To understand this, look at the concept of the Big Bang. Scientists say that the creation of the material universe began when all energy was compressed into a singularity and was then released in a giant explosion. Yet as mentioned earlier, an explosion is an outgoing force that leads to expansion without the formation of organized structures. So the Big Bang model only makes sense if there is a contracting force to balance the expansive force. Only by balancing expansion, can a specific form be created and maintained over time.

The Power of Self

Image 7 - The first sphere in the void

The masters say that the Creator defined an extension of its own Being, namely the basic cosmic energy that would be used as the building material for the world of form. This created the very first polarity, namely a polarity between the Creator, representing the masculine, expansive element, and the Ma-ter light, representing the feminine, contracting element. This is somewhat similar to concepts found in some religions, such as the Taoist concepts of Yin and Yang.

Another way to say this is that the outgoing force represents consciousness. A self-aware being can formulate a mental image of the form it wants to create. It can then superimpose or project this mental image upon the Ma-ter light, which then takes on the matrix of the envisioned form. Thus, we might say that the active element of creation is consciousness, which causes the passive element, energy, to take on specific forms.

After having defined the Ma-ter light, the Creator then projected the Ma-ter light out from the singularity, and it created the first sphere in the void. The void was empty, but the first sphere contained energy that vibrated within a certain spectrum of vibrations.

THE CREATION OF SELF-AWARE BEINGS

After having created this first sphere, the Creator then defined certain structures in the sphere. It did so by forming an image in its mind and projecting or superimposing it upon the Ma-ter light. As a rough illustration, we can compare the Ma-ter light to a movie screen. It has no image in itself, but it is capable of reflecting any image projected upon it.

4 | How the world of form was created

As the next step, the Creator created a number of self-aware beings and sent or projected them into the first sphere. These beings were created out of the Creator's own Being, which is why they had self-awareness. Yet their self-awareness was not the omnipresent awareness of the Creator; it was a localized self-awareness. These first beings saw themselves as individual beings, which gave them the opportunity to start with a localized self-awareness and gradually expand it, until they reached the level of the Creator while still remaining individual beings. The purpose that the Creator has in creating a world of form is to create more Creators, which also causes the Creator to grow.

The first beings started out with a localized sense of self, being focused on the environment in which they lived, an environment created for them by the Creator. It would be rather scary for a new being to start out in a void. How would a newly created being be able to imagine structures and create them itself? So a new being starts out in a predefined environment, and it then gradually learns about its own creative abilities within that environment. As the being expands its awareness of its creative abilities, it can even start changing its environment according to its own vision.

This is a principle that applies to all self-aware beings in a world of form, including ourselves. All beings start out with a localized sense of self, and they start out in a predefined environment. By responding to their environment, they gradually learn about their creative abilities. All self-aware beings have the same basic creative abilities as the Creator— but not to the same degree. They have the ability to formulate a mental image and then project that image upon the Ma-ter light, causing the light to take on the actual or physical form of the image.

All self-aware beings also have complete free will, which means they have the ability to formulate any mental image they can imagine. They also have the ability and the right to project any image they can imagine upon the Ma-ter light. However, because beings live inside a certain environment, they will inevitably experience – as their physical environment – the images they project upon the Ma-ter light. It is precisely by formulating images, making decisions about which images to project upon the

Ma-ter light, and then experiencing the consequences of this process that we grow in self-awareness.

THE SUCCESSION OF SPHERES

Let us return to the first sphere. The beings in that sphere started out by exploring their creative abilities, gradually gaining mastery over their environment and starting to define their own environment. Yet as they did this, they also explored their inherent sense that they were extensions of a greater Being. As they became more aware of their connection to the Creator, they started building a sense of oneness with the Creator.

As each individual being attained this oneness, it became aware that "If the Creator is my source, then all other beings in my sphere must come from the same source." Thus, vertical oneness became horizontal oneness, and all beings in the first sphere started feeling at one with each other, while still retaining their individuality (actually, attaining true individuality as being part of a larger whole).

As the beings in the first sphere attained this oneness, they were able to accelerate the energy used to construct the first sphere (raise its vibration). This is a process whereby the entire sphere ascended to a higher state, in which it became obvious that the sphere was made from the Creator's Being. Thus, while the beings still saw themselves as individual beings, it was no longer possible to believe that they were separated from the Creator or from each other. And it was no longer possible to believe that the first sphere was made from a substance that was separated from the Creator or had an existence of its own. The first sphere had then become a permanent part of what we, from our perspective, call the spiritual realm.

After the beings in the first sphere had caused their sphere to ascend, they had attained a level of mastery. They were not at the same level of self-awareness as the Creator, but they had risen far beyond where they started. In order to give these beings an opportunity to expand their mastery, the Creator then defined a second sphere in the void.

4 | *How the world of form was created*

Yet instead of creating structures in the second sphere, the Creator allowed the ascended masters from the first sphere to create the structures in the second sphere. And instead of sending extensions of itself into the second sphere, the Creator allowed the masters from the first sphere to create extensions of their own beings, and then send them into the environment they had created in the second sphere. Thus, the masters from the first sphere became the "gods" or the spiritual parents for the beings in the second sphere.

This process of creating a new sphere when the previous sphere ascended has continued. The masters say that the material universe is in the seventh of these spheres. It is important to understand that for each time a new sphere is defined, the base energy for that sphere is more dense than it was for the previous sphere. This, means that the energy makes it seem more likely for the beings in the sphere that the sphere is separated from the Creator and exists on its own. This explains why it is currently possible to believe in the two classical illusions known to humanity:

- Traditional religion, which says that there is a God, but it is a remote God up there in the sky. The material world is separated from God's kingdom by a barrier, and we can cross it only with the help of some foreign element that is controlled by the external religion.

- Materialism, which says that there is no God and that matter can exist on its own, meaning it needs nothing beyond itself in order to exist. Thus, the material universe was not created by an intelligent being according to a pre-conceived plan. It came into being through an entirely materialistic process, driven by random events and a set of natural laws that no one defined.

Both of these illusions are built upon the deeper illusion created by the limited range of our physical senses. We can detect only the vibrations within the spectrum that makes up matter. We cannot directly see that matter is part of a greater continuum of vibrations, making it seem believable to us that matter is all there is, that matter exists on its own or that matter is separated from Spirit. The path of the mystic is a process of raising our consciousness, until we have direct, mystical experiences that shatter the believability of this primal human illusion.

INTRODUCING SPIRITUAL RAYS

We have already seen that we can take Einstein's famous formula and apply simple math, whereby we get this new formula:

$$\frac{E}{c^2} = m$$

As mentioned, this formula shows us that the material universe was created from energy of a higher vibration, and this energy was then reduced by a certain factor. Yet what Einstein defined as c^2 was only the latest out of several such reduction factors.

The ascended masters teach that the sphere in which we live is created from spiritual light that has been reduced in vibration by a total of seven reduction factors. These factors can also be described as seven types of spiritual energies, and it is the combination of these seven energies that makes up the material frequency spectrum.

These seven types of energies are what the ascended masters call the seven rays. The masters teach that everything in the material universe is made from a combination of all seven rays. For example, planet earth was created by seven spiritual beings, called the Elohim. These beings came together in the spiritual realm and combined their creative efforts to define a mental blueprint for our planet. Once the blueprint was defined, they then began the process of gradually superimposing the blueprint upon the Ma-ter light. And the driving force in this process was the energies and qualities of the seven rays. This happened partially through the power of sound, where the Elohim used specific sounds to produce rhythmic vibrations, that gradually caused the energies to take on the form of their blueprint. (In the beginning was the Word, and the Word was with God and the Word was God.)

| 4 | *How the world of form was created*

While this may sound like a linear process, it was in reality more complex. However, what is important for us is that the seven rays can be said to form seven layers of vibrations that "separate" the energies of the material world from the spiritual realm. So when we attempt to look at the spiritual world, it is as if there are seven veils that separate us from a clear vision of the spiritual realm—we are looking through seven panes of colored glass. As long as our consciousness is affected by the illusion of separation, we cannot see through the energies of the seven rays, which means we cannot gain a clear vision of the spiritual realm. We see only the colored glass panes in the kaleidoscope of Self.

This means that the path of raising our consciousness towards the mastery of Self is a process of working our way up through the seven rays, starting with the first ray and ending with the seventh.

By passing the initiations of the ray, we actually attune our minds to the ray and become one with its vibration.

As we pass the initiations of the first ray, we actually attune our minds to the first ray and become one with its vibration (or we can also say that our minds begin to vibrate in sync with the first ray). As this attunement happens, the first ray will no longer form a veil that obscures our vision. Instead, we will be able to see through the energies of the first ray and gain a clearer vision of the spiritual side of life. We will also become an open door for the energies of the first ray to stream through the Self, which means we will increase the power of Self.

This process can then continue through all seven rays, until we begin to see the underlying oneness behind all visible phenomena. We can now see through the veils, and thus we see oneness behind diversity. This is what the ascended masters call Christ consciousness. This process will gradually give us complete mastery over the matter realm, meaning we can indeed do the kind of works that Jesus did. We can formulate purer images and superimpose them upon the Ma-ter light, whereby we can override the impure images that we currently see outpictured as limitations on earth, such as disease or limited resources.

The path of initiation under the seven rays is led by specific ascended masters, called the Chohans. A Chohan is a master who is the "head teacher" for a particular ray. We will later take a closer look at the rays and the path of initiation, the Path of the Seven Veils.

FOUR LEVELS OF THE WORLD

In order to set a better foundation for the coming chapters, we will add one more layer of complexity. As has been explained, a new sphere starts out by being made of energies of a certain vibrational level. As the self-aware beings who inhabit the sphere raise their consciousness, they also raise the vibration of their sphere, until it ascends and becomes part of the spiritual realm.

In other words, when a sphere is created, a base energy is defined. This is the lowest or most dense energy found in that sphere. As has also been said, for each new sphere, the base energy is more dense than for the previous sphere. This means that for our sphere, there is a rather large gap between the base energy and the energy of the spiritual realm.

It simply is not possible to step down energy directly from the vibrational level of the spiritual realm to the vibrational level of our base energy. Furthermore, even if it was possible, there was no way that beings in the material realm could ever ascend to the spiritual realm if they had to cross such a huge gap in vibration. Thus, the stepping-down process is accomplished in four stages. This means there are four divisions, sometimes called "octaves," in the material sphere. Let us give a rough description of the four levels by comparing them to the construction of a building.

| 4 | How the world of form was created

4 LEVELS OF THE MATERIAL UNIVERSE	
1. The etheric level or identity level	This is the highest level, where you find the mental blueprints for all forms in the material sphere. You might compare it to the level of an architect, who holds the vision for the overall design of a building.
2. The mental level	This is where you find more concrete plans for how things can actually be manifest. This compares to the level of engineers, who make more concrete and detailed plans for how to actually construct the building.
3. The emotional level	This is where you have the plans of the financial backers and owners of the building. They make the actual decision to start the building process, thereby setting the wheels in motion.
4. The physical level	This is where you find the work plans for the actual, physical labour of constructing the building.

The short explanation is that the four levels of the material realm correspond to four levels of your mind: the identity level, the mental level, the emotional level and the physical level. In order to unlock the full powers of self, you must purify these four levels of the mind from the elements that block spiritual light from flowing freely through your mind. I will shortly describe how to do this.

WE ARE EXTENSIONS OF THE MASTERS

We are designed to be co-creators. Our world was created by ascended masters, residing in the level of the spiritual realm that is right above ours. We are extensions of the masters, and we were sent here to co-create our world from the inside, eventually raising it to become part of the spiritual realm. Thus, our minds have the abilities to fulfill this mission.

We co-create by using the basic energies represented by the seven spiritual rays. The path outlined by the ascended masters can be described by saying that each ray forms a veil. As we climb the path, we gain mastery over one ray after another. We learn to use the creative energies of that ray, and we attune our minds to the vibrations of the ray. When we have gone through all seven rays, we have unlocked the full power of Self.

What complicates the picture is that there is a huge gap in vibration between the spiritual and the material realm. Thus, the process of stepping down spiritual energy to the material level was accomplished in four stages. As a result of this, we have layers in our minds, corresponding to the four levels: identity, thoughts, emotions and physical. For most people the higher levels of the mind are beyond conscious awareness. It is in these subconscious layers that we have accumulated the blocks that obstruct our creative powers—the glass pieces in the kaleidoscope of self.

As we walk the path of the seven rays, we will clear out the blocks in the four layers of the mind. Thus, walking the path of the ascended masters is a two-fold process of clearing out the blocks in the four layers of the mind while attaining mastery of the seven spiritual rays. As we complete this process, we will unlock our natural power of Self. We can then fulfill the reason for which we chose to come into this world, namely to help co-create a world that is far beyond what we currently see on earth.

PART TWO

A PRACTICAL APPROACH TO SPIRITUAL GROWTH

CHAPTER 5

FUNDAMENTAL QUESTIONS ABOUT SELF

If you are open to this book, you are what is commonly called a seeker or a spiritual seeker. I remember how, even as a young child, I always wanted answers to the big questions of life. I wanted to know how the world really works and I wanted to know why I am here. I simply couldn't live without having answers to these questions, so I kept searching until I found the teachings of the ascended masters—and I am still always open to deeper answers. You have probably gone through your own journey that led you to this point.

What I will do in this chapter is to look at how the teachings of the ascended masters can provide answers to the big questions in life, often called the fundamental questions. I am not saying this will be final answers, as the coming chapters will reveal deeper layers and nuances. But we can still suggest answers that go beyond what we find in most religious or spiritual teachings.

WHO AM I? WHAT IS THE SELF?

As we have seen, science has revealed that energy is a deeper layer of reality than matter. Galaxies and toasters are both made from atoms. Yet galaxies and toasters do not produce atoms; it is the atoms that produce galaxies and toasters. Atoms are made from elementary particles, and these are made from energy waves. In other words, matter does not produce energy; energy produces matter.

| 5 | *Fundamental questions about Self*

We all know that our brains are made of matter and our thoughts are obviously made from energy waves. Thus, it simply is not logical that the gray matter between our ears can produce consciousness. Consciousness can be seen as a stream that enters the material world from a higher realm. Our minds are – more or less – open doors for this stream of consciousness. Obviously, our physical brains can indeed alter our state of consciousness, and the brain does give rise to much of what we normally call thoughts. However, the effect of the brain is more like the colored filters you put in front of stage lights. They do not produce the white light; they simply alter its color.

The ascended masters make a distinction between the mind or consciousness and thoughts and feelings. The mind is the container and thoughts are the contents. The brain can indeed affect our thoughts, even produce some thoughts, but the brain does not produce consciousness. Your are not your thoughts; you are your mind, your container of self.

So you are not a material being and your self-awareness is not a product of the physical matter in your brain. Instead, you are a non-material being who is only using the body and the brain for a twofold purpose, namely to experience the material world from the inside and to express your creative abilities in this world.

WHERE DID THE SELF COME FROM?

The ascended masters say we are spiritual beings who have descended into our physical bodies. Yet we are not separate beings; we are extensions of beings in the spiritual realm. These beings have created the material world and the basic structures in this world. Yet they have done their creation from the outside. We are then sent here to continue the creative process from the inside—we are designed to be co-creators with our spiritual parents.

The identity that makes you a unique individual is the extension of your higher self or spiritual self, which we will take a closer look at in a later chapter. Of course, our spiritual parents are the offspring or extensions of spiritual beings in a higher sphere, and this hierarchy or Chain of Being goes all the way to the Creator.

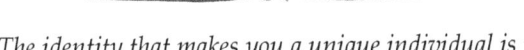

The identity that makes you a unique individual is the extension of your higher self or spiritual self.

The ascended masters say what some mystics have been saying for thousands of years, namely that there truly is only one Self, namely the Self of the Creator. Everything is created from this one Self or one mind, and thus nothing is truly separated from the one mind. We have been given a portion or spark of this one mind, and this is what gives us self-awareness. We have the potential to expand this self-awareness while still retaining individuality, yet we cannot do that as separate beings. We can do it only by seeing ourselves as part of the greater whole—the one mind.

On the overall level, you are created as an individualized extension of the Creator's Being. You were created with a localized, point-like sense of self-awareness, and your purpose is to expand that self-awareness, until you reach the same level of awareness as the Creator that created you. At that point, you can either enter the Allness, or you can become a Creator, creating your own world of form. So this addresses, in a general way, why you exist as a individual being with self-awareness.

On another level, we can consider why you are here in the material world and what your purpose is for being here. At this level, you are an extension of your spiritual self. You were created to serve as a co-creator with your spiritual self and your spiritual parents. So you are meant to help raise the vibration of the material realm, until the entire sphere can ascend and become part of the spiritual realm.

Yet the real purpose is actually your growth in self-awareness. The material world is simply an environment that is designed as a kind of

| 5 | *Fundamental questions about Self*

theater or laboratory in which self-aware beings can expand their sense of self. Our spiritual parents have defined an external environment, and we are meant to use that environment to expand our awareness of our creative, or rather co-creative, abilities.

We can then gradually attain mastery over our environment, so that we can build upon the foundation set by our spiritual parents. As we attain this mastery, we will gain the mastery of mind over matter, and when this process is complete, we can ascend to the spiritual realm and become ascended masters. From there, we can choose to move on to other realms of learning, or we can remain with the earth and seek to help unascended beings grow.

WHAT IS MY RELATIONSHIP WITH GOD?

As already made clear, the ascended masters say there is a God, but the God of the ascended masters is very different from a traditional Christian image of God. The Creator is nothing like the angry, judgmental and remote God who will send us to hell if we displease him. Even though the ascended masters rarely talk about the Old Testament, they do say that the first two of the ten commandments give us an important clue as to how to develop a better view of God.

The first commandment says: "Thou shalt have no other gods before me," which means we should never allow any man-made "god" (or religion) to stand between us and a direct, mystical experience of the ultimate God. This ties in with the second commandment, which says: "Thou shalt not take unto thyself any graven image." The masters say this does not only refer to an idol made of wood, stone or gold. Its deeper meaning is any mental image that ascribes form to God. According to the ascended masters, the Creator is the source of all form, but as such, the Creator is completely beyond form.

We human beings have a tendency to use what we can perceive in the visible world to reason about what is in the invisible world. This is especially non-constructive when it comes to God. There is literally nothing – no "thing" – in the world of form that can accurately depict

The Power of Self

the Creator who is beyond form. Yet if we fixate our minds on a particular mental image of God, then this fixation will block our minds from having a mystical experience of the real Creator. The nature of a mystical experience is that it takes us beyond our current mental box. So if we insist on a mystical experience conforming to the images and beliefs inside our mental box, our minds simply cannot be free to have an experience that is outside the box.

The Creator is the source of all form, but as such, the Creator is completely beyond form.

It is indeed possible for a human being to have an experience of the Creator's Being. Yet once one has had such an experience, it becomes obvious that it is utterly pointless to seek to describe the Creator through words or images from this world.

What is your relationship with the Creator? Well, you are an extension of the Creator, thus you are part of the Creator's total Being. This means the real God does not judge you. The Creator has given you a part of its own Being, and then it has given you complete and total free will as to what you do with that part. A judgmental and controlling God would never give you such freedom. Thus, the real God is a God who loves you with a love that is completely beyond the conditional love known to most of us here on earth. And does it not make sense that the Creator who is beyond form, loves you with a love that is beyond conditions?

WHERE AM I GOING; WHAT HAPPENS AFTER DEATH?

Again, this question can be answered on several levels. On the overall level, you are a Creator in the making. Thus, you are engaged in a process of expanding your self-awareness, until you reach the level of a Creator.

However, on a more immediate level, your task is to attain mastery in the environment of the material universe, specifically planet earth. Once

| 5 | *Fundamental questions about Self*

you have this mastery, you can ascend to the spiritual realm and become an ascended master. So the more immediate concern is how to master your co-creative abilities and qualify for your ascension, which we will address in coming chapters.

What does it actually mean to master your environment? The ascended masters say that Jesus, and many other spiritual teachers, came to demonstrate the potential we all have. Jesus' so-called miracles were not miracles at all. They were demonstrations of the mastery of mind over matter that we can all attain, as we walk the path towards the ascension. That is why Jesus said that those who believe on him shall do the works that he did, even greater works.

Based on this, most of us can probably look at our own lives and say: "Well, I'm not quite there yet." And this brings up the question of what happens to us after our physical body dies. The ascended masters say that we, of course, do not die when our bodies die. We, as self-aware beings, do indeed survive death and enter a different realm. This leads to the question: "If you are not ready for the ascension when your body dies, then what happens?"

The answer given by the ascended masters is that you will receive a chance to go back in another physical body, and this process will continue for as many lifetimes as necessary, until you qualify for your ascension. This is, of course, the process that is commonly known as reincarnation.

The masters say that when the earth was first created, it was in a higher and purer state than today. The first waves of beings that took embodiment here descended in a higher state of consciousness than what is considered "normal" today. As a result, they needed only one lifetime to qualify for their ascensions.

After a majority of the people on earth descended to the lower state of consciousness we see today, many forms of imbalances came to be manifest, and as a result, it became impossible to maintain a physical body for the original life-span. Due to this and the fact that the lower state of consciousness makes it more difficult to qualify for the ascension, it was no longer possible for most beings to ascend in one lifetime. Thus, reincarnation became a necessity.

WHY IS REINCARNATION IMPORTANT

One reason reincarnation is important is that it explains certain questions that are otherwise difficult to deal with. Most spiritually interested people are probably aware that the human psyche is very complex, but where did this complexity come from?

According to a materialistic philosophy, there could have been nothing before the physical body, so the common explanation is that our psyches are a combination of inherited traits and environmental influences. Yet how does this explain that some people have much more complex psyches than others or that some are far more evil than others?

As an example, look at some of the most evil people in history. Many of them did not have evil parents and experienced no extraordinary trauma during childhood. An obvious explanation is that such people are reincarnations of older beings that developed psychological issues over many lifetimes. This will also explain why any person who starts working on their own psychology will uncover an extensive complexity, with many layers of the subconscious mind.

It is much easier for sincere seekers to walk the path towards a higher state of consciousness by acknowledging, that we are very complex beings because we have evolved over many lifetimes. Thus, we cannot expect that progress on the path can be made without dealing with the many layers of the psyche. And this makes it far easier for us to develop a realistic, long-term approach to the path, rather than falling prey to the many quick-fix approaches offered in the spiritual marketplace. We will return to this later, when we take a closer look at the path, but it is important to be aware of reincarnation as we begin to study the practical aspects of the path.

CHAPTER 6

HOW TO ANCHOR YOURSELF FIRMLY ON THE PATH

As I said, many ascended masters have been in embodiment on earth, so they know this is a difficult planet with a rather dense mass consciousness. Although they are committed to helping each person on earth, the masters know that there are so many levels of consciousness, that they cannot take the same approach to all people. In fact, the masters know there are many people that they simply cannot help directly.

If you take a look at humanity, it is not hard to see that some people are in a state of mind, where they feel they are victims and feel like they are always fighting someone else. Such people are not open to the ascended masters and their teachings, so they simply have to learn by seeing how the cosmic mirror returns to them what they are sending out. This is what the masters call the "School of Hard Knocks."

You can also see that many people are open to a religious teaching, but they are not ready for what I call the mystical approach. The masters can help such people by giving them an outer teaching, but in most cases people turn it into a formal, closed-minded religion that is far from the real path of self-transcendence. Such a religion usually makes the promise that you can be saved by fulfilling certain outer requirements, such as being a member of a certain church or declaring Jesus to be your lord and savior. Yet until people have had enough of following an outer religion and want something more, the masters cannot help them in a more direct way.

The Power of Self

It is not the intent here to set up some elitist value-judgment, saying that some people are more advanced than others. Yet it must be recognized that some people are ready for a direct relationship with the ascended masters and others are not ready. What is the dividing line? You must have come to the point, where you recognize one simple truth: "If I want to change my outer circumstances, I have to start by changing my inner circumstances. If I want to change the world, I have to start by changing myself."

In order to get to that point, you have to take responsibility for your own spiritual growth, even your own salvation. You have to acknowledge a truth that Jesus actually explained, but which most Christians have "overlooked." As we have seen, the mystical path is a process of overcoming the illusion that you are separated from your source. It is a process of coming into oneness with something greater than your self. And the key to completing this process is to change your sense of self, to change your state of consciousness. You must transcend the self that sees itself as a separate being, and you must be reborn as a Self that sees itself as an extension of a greater being.

The bottom line is this: your circumstances here on earth are a reflection of your state of consciousness. The key to changing your circumstances is to change your state of consciousness. The key to finding the exit from the human maze and ascending from earth is to change your state of consciousness. Once you accept this, you are ready for a more direct teaching from the ascended masters. If you had not been at that point, you probably would not have found this book, and you definitely would not still be reading it. So let us simply acknowledge this and then move on to how you can anchor yourself on the path offered by the ascended masters.

THE INITIAL TRIAL PERIOD

As I said, in order to find the ascended masters, you have to be willing to change yourself, your state of consciousness. Of course, being willing to change is not the same as having already changed. The ascended masters

| 6 | *How to anchor yourself firmly on the path*

are teachers, so they do not require their students to be perfect; they require us to be willing to learn. The importance of this is that when most of us hear about ascended masters, we have reached a certain level of maturity, but we are still dragging along a lot of baggage from this and past lifetimes. So we will have to go through an initial period, where we make an effort to get rid of some of this baggage.

Thus, it is perfectly normal that in the beginning we will have various issues to deal with. There might be certain aspects of the masters' teachings that we find it difficult to accept, there may be certain recommendations that we find it difficult to apply and there may be certain behaviors or habits that we find it difficult to leave behind. Yet if we do follow the path offered by the masters, we will – and often after a relatively short period of time – come to feel that although we are not home free, we have certainly anchored ourselves firmly on the upward path. We have a clear vision of where we are going and what it takes to get there, and we know that if we keep applying ourselves, we will reach our goal. So what will it take to get to that point?

THE TWO "LEGS" OF THE PATH

As we have seen, we live in a world where everything is created from energy that has been made to take on specific forms. Thus, your higher potential, your natural state, is that your mind, your self, is an open door for light from a higher realm. You exercise the power of Self by forming a mental vision of what you want to create and then superimposing it upon the light streaming through your mind. It is now obvious that the more light you have streaming through your mind, the greater will be your creative powers. However, in order to open your mind to a greater flow of light, you must clear away the elements that block the light from entering.

There are two elements that block the flow of light through your mind. They are the limiting beliefs that reside in the four levels of your mind and the misqualified energies that accumulate in these four levels of your energy field. Thus, the two legs of progress are to study

The Power of Self

appropriate teachings (spirituality, psychology, self-help etc.) in order to see through all limiting beliefs and to practice spiritual techniques in order to overcome the misqualified energies. However, it isn't quite that simple.

Studying spiritual teachings does not mean to study them as you study a topic in a university. The ascended masters are not interested in having you become an A student who can recite by heart certain teachings. What the masters are looking for is that you have a mystical experience, an "Aha experience" that truly shifts your consciousness. It is quite possible to study the teachings of the ascended masters for decades without having such an experience. Yet students who do this usually acquire such a great intellectual understanding of the teachings, that it causes them to feel pride that they know so much. And this pride can block the Aha experience, thereby blocking progress.

There are two elements that block the flow of light through your mind—the limiting beliefs and the misqualified energies accumulated in your energy field.

It is, therefore, important to approach the study of spiritual teachings with the awareness that the real purpose is to achieve an Aha experience. And that means you need to make an effort to look for your prejudices, the beliefs that your ego does not want you to question. The equation is very simple. The insight that will shift your consciousness is *not* found within the mental box of your present beliefs—if it was, your consciousness would already have shifted.

So you can find the insight only by looking outside the box of your current beliefs. And that means you must be open to ideas that challenge or go beyond your current beliefs. So if you study the teachings of the ascended masters for the purpose of having certain beliefs validated, you simply will not get Aha experiences. And that really means there is no purpose in studying the teachings. Which means that instead of continuing to study, you need to do something different.

THE IMPORTANCE OF INVOKING LIGHT

There are millions of people in the modern world who have already studied some spiritual teaching. There are millions who have already practiced a spiritual technique. How can such people benefit from what the ascended masters offer? What do the masters have that is different from what is found elsewhere?

Well, many of the techniques that modern spiritual people practice have come from the East, and they often take the form of meditation, yoga or in some cases chanting. The ascended masters are in no way diminishing the value of such practice, but they do suggest that many people in the modern world, could benefit immensely from practicing a technique pioneered by the ascended masters. That technique is to invoke spiritual light through the power of the sacred word, the spoken word.

The seven Elohim used a rhythmic application of sound in order to make the Ma-ter light take on the form of the physical earth.

I earlier mentioned that the seven Elohim used a rhythmic application of sound in order to make the Ma-ter light take on the form of the physical earth. We are all meant to be co-creators with the Elohim, and how can we do this unless we learn to use the same technique that the Elohim used for creating the earth?

It is, of course, possible to cause the Ma-ter light to take on form through the power of thought. Yet in today's world, there is so much misqualified energy and so many limiting ideas, that it is very difficult for a student to achieve clarity of mind by using meditation alone. In fact, for many Westerners, seeking to still the mind can actually open you up to misqualified energy and impure thoughts from the mass consciousness. This is the main reason why some people have experienced having positive effects of meditation for a time, only to then start a negative slide leading to less results or even negative experiences.

The ascended masters explain that in today's very intense energetic conditions, it is extremely important to use the most powerful tool available to us, and that tool is our voice, the spoken word. When you are surrounded by lower energies, your first task truly is to create a protected sphere around your mind and energy field, so you are not overwhelmed by the energy from your surroundings. And there simply is no more efficient way of doing this than using the spoken word through the decrees and invocations given to us directly by the ascended masters.

THE MASS CONSCIOUSNESS

So far, we have not talked much about the mass consciousness, but we have seen that all life is connected. That connection is obviously a connection in consciousness. We have even seen that as you go towards the deeper layers of the subatomic world, you encounter a field of consciousness. So it is not hard to envision that all human beings are connected through a common consciousness, or a collective energy field. And when you consider the bloody history of humankind – even in the short interval that we call recorded history – you see that there could be – there *must* be – a substantial amount of misqualified energy accumulated in this collective field.

In the collective field you also find all of the illusions that spring from the consciousness of separation and duality. And if you have accepted any of these illusions – which is virtually impossible to avoid for any of us – then those illusions will be like open doors in your personal energy field, through which the misqualified energies from the collective field can enter.

| 6 | *How to anchor yourself firmly on the path*

This influence from the collective consciousness can explain many phenomena in our personal lives. Why do we have some days where we simply feel low or depressed, often for no obvious outer reason? Is it because on those days we are exposed to a more intense invasion of energy from the mass mind? Is it possible that the energies from the collective field can overwhelm people and cause depression, addictions or mental illness? Is it possible that these energies can cause people to become discouraged, so they give up on the spiritual path, even give up on life?

The ascended masters teach that most spiritual people are highly sensitive. The upside is that this is why we are open to the spiritual side of life. Yet the downside is that this can also make us more open to the energies in the mass consciousness. Unless you have what the masters call discernment, you will be open to both higher and lower energies—sensitivity is sensitivity. Thus, it is extremely important to use proper techniques to seal your energy field from the mass consciousness, so that you can create a protected sphere that enables you to actually hear your own thoughts instead of the "static" of the mass consciousness. Many people have experienced that the most effective way to establish this spiritual protection is precisely the spoken word. Many spiritual people will recognize one or more of the following scenarios:

- You feel that you are in a state of inner chaos, where your mind is confused or agitated to the point, where you cannot relax or find any kind of peace.

- You feel discouraged, perhaps even depressed, because you feel like nothing you do makes a difference or has any higher purpose.

- You feel confused, feel like you have no clear vision or sense of what your purpose is.

- You feel like there is an external force seeking to invade your mind and take over your thoughts and emotions.

- You feel like there are certain people who are seeking to control you, and you feel powerless to withstand their control. Or you feel like you constantly have to spend energy defending yourself.

Now consider that all of these – and many similar – phenomena could have a common cause: your energy field is unprotected from the energies coming from other people or the mass consciousness. This external energy is what makes you feel agitated, overwhelmed or depressed. Thus, the one major thing that could give you a new direction in life would be to learn how to do two things:

- Seal your energy field effectively from the energy fields of other people and the mass consciousness.

- Remove the misqualified energy that has already accumulated in your personal field.

We might consider this energetic hygiene, and for many ascended master students, invoking spiritual light for protection and transmutation has become a part of their daily routine, a part that is as important and natural as taking a shower. You are taking care of your energy body as you are taking care of your physical body, you simply use different techniques for taking care of the different bodies. You use certain forms of light to invoke body armor around your energy body, and you use other forms of energy to take a violet flame shower.

UNDERSTANDING DARK FORCES

While this book will not go into great depth about dark forces, it is important to realize that besides the mass consciousness, there are also certain forces on this planet who will seek to influence and control you in a more aggressive way. The ascended masters tell us to not be afraid of dark forces, but to not be blind to their existence either. The masters talk about two types of dark forces:

- We earlier looked at the fact that, starting with the fourth sphere, some beings fell into the duality consciousness. Some of these fallen beings have been allowed to come to earth, and some are in physical embodiment while others are associated with the earth in the emotional, mental and lower identity realm.

- Dark forces that were created in the material world by concentrating negative energy to the point, where it attains a rudimentary form of consciousness.

There are two main reason why it is important to know about the existence of dark forces with an aggressive intent. One is that it explains why people can commit the inhumane and atrocious acts we have witnessed during history and even in today's world. For example, a young man who goes into a school and starts shooting at people is not acting from a normal state of consciousness. His mind has been taken over by dark forces, and their purpose is to steal the light of all people affected by an atrocity.

Dark forces cannot influence people against their free will. Thus, they have to somehow deceive us into inviting them into our energy fields.

That being said, it is also important to realize that dark forces cannot influence people against their free will. Thus, they have to somehow deceive us into inviting them into our energy fields. Many people do this without knowing what they are doing, but as a spiritual student it is obviously important to become aware of the existence of dark forces, so you can protect yourself from their influence.

The other reason why it is important to be aware of dark forces is that it allows you to invoke spiritual light in order to seal your energy field from such forces and the energies they project at you. You can also invoke spiritual light in order to cut yourself free from any forces that might already have gained an inroad into your mind and energy field. You can find more information about dark forces on my websites or in some of my other books. The important point for this book is to add the perspective, that invoking spiritual light will both protect you and cut you free from the influence of forces that aggressively seek to influence you.

The Power of Self

INVOCATIONS AND DECREES

The ascended masters have given two main tools for invoking spiritual light, namely invocations and decrees. A decree is a rhythmic affirmation that has several verses and they generally rhyme. It is usually given several times. An invocation is a longer ritual that involves affirmations interspersed with verses that are repeated. In some cases an invocation is made by interspersing the verses from a decree with affirmations.

We might say that the main difference is that a decree is designed to be the most powerful way to invoke light from a specific spiritual ray, whereas an invocation is designed to both invoke light and help you overcome limiting beliefs. A decree is often given with great power and it can be given at high speed. This creates a very powerful effect that invokes a high measure of light. An invocation is usually given more slowly, so you have time to notice the affirmations and how they help you challenge limiting beliefs and accept more empowering beliefs. A decree is focused on invoking light for a specific ray, whereas an invocation is focused on helping you transcend a specific problem, such as overcoming a spiritual crises, invoking greater abundance, clearing your four lower bodies, learning to let go of the past, loving yourself or many other such topics.

What decrees and invocations have in common is that you speak them aloud, and for many spiritual people this can take some getting used to. Many of us have, both in this and past lives, spent a lot of time in silence and meditation. We are quite comfortable about going within, but using the spoken word is an outgoing action. In the beginning, we often feel some resistance to speaking out loud, partly because we are not used to it and partly because our egos will actually seek to discourage us from invoking spiritual light. The ego knows that it can only survive in the shadows of your mind, so the more light you invoke, the less shadows will be left and thus the ego will have less places to hide.

The point is that for many people, using decrees can be the missing link for their spiritual growth. You can use the spoken word to break the bonds that have been holding you at a certain level of the path. Yet the trick is to realize, that those same bonds will resist your use of the spoken word, and thus you must be somewhat determined in order to overcome your initial resistance. Once you do break through this resistance, you will feel how the flow of light you invoke will give you a new sense of clarity, energy and eventually even a sense of inner peace and stillness. It may seem ironic that being very active is the key to inner stillness, but when you understand how chaotic energy in your personal field can rob you of inner peace, you see why it is indeed an invaluable tool to invoke light from above.

You can use the spoken word to break the bonds that have been holding you at a certain level of the path. Yet the trick is to realize, that those same bonds will resist your use of the spoken word.

How do you get started on using the spoken word? The simplest way is to visit the website *www.transcendecetoolbox.com*. There you will find a large number of decrees and invocations along with instructions and recordings that teach you how to use them.

However, one word of caution. As we have seen, there are seven spiritual rays. For each ray, there are three ascended masters who serve special functions. There is the level of the Elohim, which is the masters that created the material realm, including this planet. Then there is the level of the Archangels, which serve to bring us specific spiritual qualities, such as protection. And then there is the level of the Chohan, which is the main teacher for each ray. So you can see that for the seven rays, there is a total of 21 ascended masters that you can invoke—and this can seem quite overwhelming in the beginning.

So in order to avoid being too overwhelmed, here is a simple recommendation. What you need in order to get started is to invoke three forms of spiritual light:

The Power of Self

- You need the first ray in order to get protection, and this is best done with decrees to Archangel Michael or with invocations to Archangel Michael.

- You need the fourth ray in order to be cut free from any ties to the mass consciousness or dark forces, and for this purpose the decree to the Elohim Astrea is the most powerful.

- You need to invoke the violet flame for transmuting misqualified energy that has already entered your energy field. For this you can use any decree to the seventh ray, such as decrees to Saint Germain. Or you can use one of the many invocations that focus on a specific problem, such as forgiveness, gratitude or rising above the past.

By following a simple program of invoking the first, the fourth and the seventh ray, you will – depending on how much time you put into it – relatively soon begin to feel like you are no longer drowning in negative energy. You now have your head above the water, and you can begin to look around, or rather look within, where you will find that you can receive a clearer inner direction from your higher self or the ascended master that is working with you personally. And it is precisely such inner directions that will help you rise to a new level of your path.

These directions are always being offered to you; the only question being whether there is enough silence in your energy field that you can actually receive them with your conscious mind. One of the major benefits of using the spoken word is precisely that it becomes so much easier for your inner directions to pass through the energy in your subconscious mind, so they can reach your conscious mind. And this can truly put your life in an upward spiral.

A PRACTICAL PROGRAM

Truly, the spiritual path is individual. Your situation is unique, so it is hard to give a general recommendation that will fit all readers. Some people will know that the tools for invoking light is exactly what they need, and they will apply these tools with great determination. I personally did this when I first learned about decrees almost 30 years ago.

I was at first a bit hesitant, because I had been meditating for years. But after I overcame my initial resistance, I quickly started feeling that the time I spent on invoking light paid huge dividends. The effects I felt can be divided into three categories:

- I felt that invoking spiritual protection from Archangel Michael had the effect of sealing my energy field from negative energy. I started feeling more calm, overcoming the sense of being agitated, nervous or on edge. I felt like my thoughts were more my own and that I did not have as much of a tendency for my mind to keep going around in circles, seeking to solve some problem or other.

- I felt like invoking the light from the Elohim Astrea cut me free from all ties to lower energies or even darker forces. This also made me feel generally calmer, but the most dramatic effect was that it helped me go to sleep very quickly. For most of my life I had experienced problems going to sleep, because my mind would always be going. So I would toss and turn for 2-3 hours before I was finally so exhausted that I fell asleep. The result was that I didn't get enough rest and was sleepy the next day. After I started seriously applying the decree to Astrea, it only took a couple of weeks before I started falling asleep within 15 minutes. The effect on my life was dramatic.

- By invoking the seventh-ray energy called the violet flame, I felt how old emotional wounds began to dissolve. I had a couple of situations from my teenage years that would sometimes come up in my mind, and then I would feel the original emotional pain full force. Yet after a few weeks of sincerely invoking the violet flame, I one day realized that I could think about these situations without feeling the emotional pain. Since I had not done anything else to bring about this change, the logical explanation was that the violet flame had transmuted the energy stored in my emotional body. So when I thought about the old situations, there was no longer a reservoir of misqualified energy that could overwhelm my feelings.

Based on my personal experience, I would like to recommend a simple but effective program for people who want to make a solid start on invoking spiritual light. Below you will find three decrees that I have received directly from the ascended masters. There is a decree to Archangel Michael for protection, one to Elohim Astrea for cutting you free from the mass consciousness and one to Saint Germain for transmuting misqualified energy.

What I suggest you do is to make a firm commitment that you will use these decrees for at least three months and then evaluate the results you get. I suggest you give the decree to Archangel Michael for 15 minutes in the morning, followed by the decree to Saint Germain for 15 minutes. In the evening, you then give the decree to Astrea for 15 minutes followed by the Saint Germain decree for another 15 minutes. I know that spending an hour a day can seem like a lot for many people, but if you give it a sincere try, I am convinced you will experience such great results that you will want to keep going. It truly is the most efficient way I know of to accelerate your spiritual growth and anchor yourself firmly on the path offered by the masters.

So let me include the decrees but also encourage you to visit:

www.transcendencetoolbox.com

where you can hear a recording of the decrees. This is important in order to learn the correct pronunciation and rhythm. You can also find a link to our online store, where you can purchase and download recordings of the decrees given multiple times. Giving the decrees along with a recording is the best way to learn how to master the art of the sacred word. I think it is one of the best investments in your spiritual growth you could ever make.

Take note that I am not implying that the program I am suggesting here will be everything you will ever need. It is meant to give you a very good start for clearing out some of the worst blocks to your spiritual vision and the flow of energy. As you gain more experience, you will want to also experiment with some of the invocations that challenge limiting beliefs at the same time as invoking light. And you will, of course, also want to study the teachings of the ascended masters, which you can find in great abundance on my various websites (See the back of the book).

I strongly recommend that you start practicing the decrees as you read the rest of the book. As I have said several times, study simply isn't enough in itself. Unless you begin to invoke spiritual light, this book will be just another intellectual exercise that wont truly shift your consciousness and give you the results you desire. Remember, that the two legs of progress are to study and to invoke spiritual light.

1.01 DECREE TO ARCHANGEL MICHAEL

In the name I AM THAT I AM, Jesus Christ, I call to my I AM Presence to flow through the I Will Be Presence that I AM and give these decrees with full power. I call to beloved Archangel Michael and Faith to shield me in your wings of electric blue light, and shatter and consume all imperfect energies and dark forces, including…

[Make personal calls]

> 1. Michael Archangel, in your flame so blue,
> there is no more night, there is only you.
> In oneness with you, I am filled with your light,
> what glorious wonder, revealed to my sight.
>
> **Michael Archangel, your Faith is so strong,**
> **Michael Archangel, oh sweep me along.**
> **Michael Archangel, I'm singing your song,**
> **Michael Archangel, with you I belong.**
>
> 2. Michael Archangel, protection you give,
> within your blue shield, I ever shall live.
> Sealed from all creatures, roaming the night,
> I remain in your sphere, of electric blue light.
>
> **Michael Archangel, your Faith is so strong,**
> **Michael Archangel, oh sweep me along.**
> **Michael Archangel, I'm singing your song,**
> **Michael Archangel, with you I belong.**

The Power of Self

3. Michael Archangel, what power you bring,
as millions of angels, praises will sing.
Consuming the demons, of doubt and of fear,
I know that your Presence, will always be near.

**Michael Archangel, your Faith is so strong,
Michael Archangel, oh sweep me along.
Michael Archangel, I'm singing your song,
Michael Archangel, with you I belong.**

4. Michael Archangel, God's will is your love,
you bring to us all, God's light from Above.
God's will is to see, all life taking flight,
transcendence of self, our most sacred right.

**Michael Archangel, your Faith is so strong,
Michael Archangel, oh sweep me along.
Michael Archangel, I'm singing your song,
Michael Archangel, with you I belong.**

Coda:

With angels I soar,
as I reach for MORE.
The angels so real,
their love all will heal.
The angels bring peace,
all conflicts will cease.
With angels of light,
we soar to new height.

The rustling sound of angel wings,
what joy as even matter sings,
what joy as every atom rings,
in harmony with angel wings.

Sealing:

In the name of the Divine Mother, I fully accept that the power of these calls is used to set free the Ma-ter light, so it can outpicture the perfect vision of Christ for my own life, for all people and for the planet. In the name I AM THAT I AM, it is done! Amen.

4.01 DECREE TO ELOHIM ASTREA

In the name I AM THAT I AM, Jesus Christ, I call to my I Will Be Presence to flow through my being and give these decrees with full power. I call to beloved Mighty Astrea and Purity to cut me free from all imperfect energies and all ties to any dark forces or conditions not of the Light, including…

[Make personal calls]

1. Beloved Astrea, your heart is so true,
your Circle and Sword of white and blue,
cut all life free from dramas unwise,
on wings of Purity our planet will rise.

**Beloved Astrea, in God Purity,
accelerate all of my life energy,
raising my mind into true unity
with the Masters of love in Infinity.**

2. Beloved Astrea, from Purity's Ray,
send forth deliverance to all life today,
acceleration to Purity, I AM now free
from all that is less than love's Purity.

**Beloved Astrea, in oneness with you,
your circle and sword of electric blue,
with Purity's Light cutting right through,
raising within me all that is true.**

3. Beloved Astrea, accelerate us all,
as for your deliverance I fervently call,
set all life free from vision impure
beyond fear and doubt, I AM rising for sure.

**Beloved Astrea, I AM willing to see,
all of the lies that keep me unfree,
I AM rising beyond every impurity,
with Purity's Light forever in me.**

4. Beloved Astrea, accelerate life
beyond all duality's struggle and strife,
consume all division between God and man,
accelerate fulfillment of God's perfect plan.

**Beloved Astrea, I lovingly call,
break down separation's invisible wall,
I surrender all lies causing the fall,
forever affirming the oneness of All.**

Coda:
Accelerate into Purity, I AM real,
Accelerate into Purity, all life heal,
Accelerate into Purity, I AM MORE,
Accelerate into Purity, all will soar.

Accelerate into Purity! (3X)
Beloved Elohim Astrea.

Accelerate into Purity! (3X)
Beloved Gabriel and Hope.

Accelerate into Purity! (3X)
Beloved Serapis Bey.

Accelerate into Purity! (3X)
Beloved I AM.

Sealing:

In the name of the Divine Mother, I fully accept that the power of these calls is used to set free the Ma-ter light, so it can outpicture the perfect vision of Christ for my own life, for all people and for the planet. In the name I AM THAT I AM, it is done! Amen.

| 6 | *How to anchor yourself firmly on the path*

7.03 DECREE TO SAINT GERMAIN

In the name I AM THAT I AM, Jesus Christ, I call to my I AM Presence to flow through the I Will Be Presence that I AM and give these decrees with full power. I call to beloved Saint Germain and Portia, the other Chohans and the Maha Chohan to release flood tides of light, to consume all blocks and attachments that prevent me from becoming one with the eternal flow of the seventh ray of creative freedom and ever-transcending oneness, including…

[Make personal calls]

1. Saint Germain, your alchemy,
with violet fire now sets me free.
Saint Germain, I ever grow,
in freedom's overpowering flow.

**O Holy Spirit, flow through me,
I am the open door for thee.
O mighty rushing stream of Light,
transcendence is my sacred right.**

2. Saint Germain, your mastery,
of violet flame geometry.
Saint Germain, in you I see,
the formulas that set me free.

**O Holy Spirit, flow through me,
I am the open door for thee.
O mighty rushing stream of Light,
transcendence is my sacred right.**

3. Saint Germain, in Liberty,
I feel the love you have for me.
Saint Germain, I do adore,
the violet flame that makes all more.

**O Holy Spirit, flow through me,
I am the open door for thee.
O mighty rushing stream of Light,
transcendence is my sacred right.**

4. Saint Germain, in unity,
I will transcend duality.
Saint Germain, my self so pure,
your violet chemistry so sure.

The Power of Self

O Holy Spirit, flow through me,
I am the open door for thee.
O mighty rushing stream of Light,
transcendence is my sacred right.

5. Saint Germain, reality,
in violet light I am carefree.
Saint Germain, my aura seal,
your violet flame my chakras heal.

O Holy Spirit, flow through me,
I am the open door for thee.
O mighty rushing stream of Light,
transcendence is my sacred right.

6. Saint Germain, your chemistry,
with violet fire set atoms free.
Saint Germain, from lead to gold,
transforming vision I behold.

O Holy Spirit, flow through me,
I am the open door for thee.
O mighty rushing stream of Light,
transcendence is my sacred right.

7. Saint Germain, transcendency,
as I am always one with thee.
Saint Germain, from soul I'm free,
I so delight in being me.

O Holy Spirit, flow through me,
I am the open door for thee.
O mighty rushing stream of Light,
transcendence is my sacred right.

8. Saint Germain, nobility,
the key to sacred alchemy.
Saint Germain, you balance all,
the seven rays upon my call.

O Holy Spirit, flow through me,
I am the open door for thee.
O mighty rushing stream of Light,
transcendence is my sacred right.

Sealing:

In the name of the Divine Mother, I fully accept that the power of these calls is used to set free the Ma-ter light, so it can outpicture the perfect vision of Christ for my own life, for all people and for the planet. In the name I AM THAT I AM, it is done! Amen.

Read more about invocations and decrees and how to use them for invoking spiritual light:

www. transcendencetoolbox.com

PART THREE

KNOWING THE SELF AND ITS COMPONENTS

CHAPTER 7

MASTERING YOUR REACTIONS

Let us take a look at your life as you experience it right now. Let us say you are facing certain conditions in your life that you feel are limiting you, because they seem to have power over you. The question now becomes: "How can I transcend those conditions?"

Conventional wisdom and common experience tell us, that the only way to transcend a limitation is to change the outer condition that limits us. In other words, the only way to change our Life Experience is to change something outside ourselves.

The problem with this approach is that there are so many external conditions over which we seemingly have limited power or no power at all. In other words, the enigma of life is: How can we change our Life Experience, if we can't gain power over the external conditions that we think control our Life Experience?

What can break this stalemate, this catch-22? What if we asked a different question: "Do external things really have power over our Life Experience, or do they have power *only* to the extent that we think they do?" In other words, where is the center of power? Is it outside ourselves (meaning we might not be able to do anything about it), or is it in our own minds, meaning we *can* do something about it?"

As I said earlier, not everyone is ready for the direct teachings from the ascended masters. Being ready means that you cross a critical threshold by recognizing the fact, that you can indeed change your outer circumstances by changing your inner circumstances. Yet what is it you must do to change your inner circumstances? You must change your Life Experience.

The ascended masters teach that there is a critical difference between outer circumstances and inner circumstances; there is a difference between your life and your Life Experience. They also teach that the key to changing your outer circumstances is to begin by changing what is going on inside your mind. The reason is that what really matters to you is not the outer circumstances but how you react to those circumstances. Your Life Experience is *not* determined by outer things but by your *reaction* to those outer things. And your reaction takes place *inside* your own mind. Your reaction is – or should be – determined exclusively by factors inside your mind, meaning factors over which you can take control.

Your Life Experience is NOT determined by outer things but by your REACTION to those things.

The ascended masters teach that the key to unlocking the power of Self is to take command over how you react to anything in the material world. They also teach that once you do master your own reactions, you will indeed have the actual power to change many outer circumstances. The only limitation being the Law of Free Will, meaning that as you gain self-mastery you will not want to interfere with the free will of other people. And thus, you will not change outer conditions against their choices.

According to the ascended masters, we have all been programmed – brain-washed – to believe in a gigantic lie. This lie has two main components. One is that you simply have to react to conditions in the material world. The other is that your reaction must be determined by the external condition. The masters teach that the deeper reality is that you are a spiritual being. As we will see in a coming chapter, the core of your being cannot be affected by anything in the material world. So there is no natural law that says you have to react to the things of this world, nor

7 | Mastering your reactions

is there any law which says that your reaction must be determined by the conditions you encounter.

One of the most beautiful teachings about this point was given by Jesus, but unfortunately the vast majority of Christians have overlooked the true meaning. Think about the whole concept of turning the other cheek. Say that a person comes up to you and slaps you hard on one cheek. What would be the "normal" reaction to this? It would be the "fight or flight response," meaning that you would either become scared and seek to get away or you would become angry and hit back. So what would it actually take for you to do what Jesus said, namely to calmly stand there and allow the person to hit you on the other cheek as well? It would take that you have complete mastery over your reaction to the situation.

In order to avoid reacting like most people would, you would have to overcome the human tendency to react with fight or flight. You would have to be so in command over your own mind, that you would essentially have no reaction, at least no human reaction, to being slapped in the face. You would have to be in such command over your mind, that you simply would not allow another person to force you to go into fight or flight. You would not allow anything in the material world to determine what goes on inside your mind. This is the essential key to self-mastery, and it has been taught by the mystics of all ages. Let us take a closer look.

THE ESSENTIAL KEY TO SELF-MASTERY

You are a spiritual being. As we have said, your highest potential is that your mind becomes an open door for the energies from the spiritual realm. Let us reach back to what we talked about in previous chapters, and take a closer look at power. What truly is power? Well, since we live in a world where everything is energy, power is energy. In order to exercise any kind of power, you need to have energy as the driving force. Yet we can talk about two kinds of energy: spiritual and material.

As we have already discussed, the ultimate power of self is the spiritual energy coming from the ascended masters. Yet here is the critical difference between most religions and the teachings of the ascended masters. Most mainstream religions portray you as an essentially powerless being, who needs some kind of external savior to come and do something for you. Christianity is a prime example, where Jesus has been turned into a strange mix between Santa Claus and Superman. If you are good, you will receive gifts in this world, and eventually he will take you in his arms and fly you to heaven. In reality, Jesus came to give us an example of the potential we all have, when we unlock the power of Self.

So here is the key realization: true power will not come to you from outside yourself. The ascended masters are *not* miracle workers who will do anything for you. Instead, the ascended masters will give you the spiritual power to do something for yourself. The trick is to realize that the power you get from the masters will not and cannot come to you from a source that you see as being outside yourself. It can and will and *must* come to you from inside yourself. Meaning that you simply cannot receive this power as long as you are looking for it outside yourself.

True power will not come to you from outside yourself. The ascended masters are not miracle workers who will do anything for you. Instead, they will give you the spiritual power to do something for yourself.

Think of this another way. We have seen that your highest potential is to be an open door for power from the spiritual realm. Yet how do you become an open door? By transcending all tendency to react to the things in this world and to let your reactions be determined by the things in this world.

Again, take the example of someone hitting you on one cheek. If you react with anger or fear, you will close yourself to your higher power. What you are essentially saying is: "I got this. I know how to deal with this on my own, so I don't need any power from you guys up there." What Jesus was truly telling us is that when we transcend these human

7 | Mastering your reactions

reactionary patterns, we can avoid reacting to situations in a lower way. Instead, we can remain neutral, non-attached, open. And through this openness, spiritual power can stream through us.

You may think that turning the other cheek is an entirely passive measure, but in reality it is the most powerful thing you could possibly do. Think about it as an exchange of energy. The person hitting you is obviously in a very human state of mind, so what he is doing is directing lower energy at you, meaning energy that is already in the material spectrum. If you react with fight or flight, you will seek to counteract his material energy with your own material energy. So it's a matter of who is the strongest at projecting material energy. Yet if you remain unmoved, you allow spiritual power to stream through you, meaning that his material energy will now be met with a much more powerful spiritual energy. So who do you think comes out on top of that energy exchange?

Jesus gave us the key 2,000 years ago. He said, "I can of my own self do nothing," meaning that he realized that as long as he identified himself as a separate being, he had no power. He also said that it was the father within him who was doing the work, meaning that he recognized that power comes from a higher source, but the doorway is within ourselves.

Jesus also made the incredibly profound statement: "The kingdom of God is within you." If you truly understand this one statement, you can unlock the full power of Self. Yet in order to fully understand what Jesus meant, it can be extremely helpful to know the self and its different components. And this is what we will examine in the coming chapters. When you see who or what the self is, you will also see how to unlock its true power.

CHAPTER 8

THE SELF IN THE SPIRITUAL REALM

Let us summarize what we have said about the creation of the world of form. The ascended masters teach that the material universe exists within the latest in a series of spheres created in the original void. Each sphere has been created with a more dense vibration than the previous ones, which means we live in what is the most dense sphere created so far. The importance is that when spiritual beings take on physical bodies on earth, we go through a dramatic shift in how we perceive our surroundings.

Take for example the common perception that we live in a world of solid matter. As we have said earlier, matter is not solid at all; it is made from vibrating energy. Yet the perception apparatus of our physical bodies simply cannot detect the vibrations, and thus "matter" appears solid and difficult to change.

As we have said, we descend in order to help raise the vibration of our sphere, until it too becomes part of the spiritual realm. And as a sphere is raised, the vibration of "matter" becomes less dense, meaning matter will appear less solid, more etherial. Right now, planet earth is at a rather low vibration, but as it is raised, it will become possible, even with the bodily senses, to perceive that matter is not self-existing. It is indeed made from finer energies, which means this world is an extension of a higher world, not a self-contained unit.

When we enter a physical body, we inevitably go through a certain "forgetting," where we lose awareness of who we really are as spiritual beings. There is nothing wrong or sinister about this, as it is indeed part

| 8 | *The Self in the spiritual realm*

of the design. As we have seen, the purpose of the world of form is the growth in self-awareness of individual extensions of the Creator. We grow by starting out with a limited sense of Self and then gradually expanding it.

When we enter a physical body, we inevitably go through a certain "forgetting," where we lose awareness of who we really are as spiritual beings.

Descending into this dense material world is indeed a major growth opportunity. We are meant to come here and lose awareness of ourselves as spiritual beings. However, in the ideal scenario, we will never lose the sense that we are connected to something outside the sense of self we have in this world. We will never forget that we are extensions of something greater, and we will never lose our longing back to the greater sense of self we had before we descended.

Descending into a limited sense of self is indeed an opportunity to expand the greater Self. When we descend, we take on a sense of self that is adapted to the conditions we find in this world. As mentioned, the senses of the physical body make matter appear solid and difficult to change, and that makes it seem believable that we are limited by the conditions in the matter world. It is by gradually awakening from this limited sense of self – and gaining mastery over the matter realm – that we grow in self-awareness.

As will be explained in more detail later, the growth in self-awareness is only possible because we have free will. So the Self that descends into the material world does indeed have free will. Yet in exercising our free will, we must do so based on our current perception. Thus, once we have descended into the material realm, we begin to make decisions based on the sense of self and the perception we have in this world—as opposed to the much broader perspective we had as spiritual beings.

The Power of Self

This opens up the possibility that we can begin to make decisions based on the perception or belief that matter does have power over us. We can therefore gradually build a sense of self that causes us to lose the sense that we are connected to something greater. We can gradually forget our longing for another realm beyond the material, and we can even begin to deny that we are spiritual beings, accepting a disempowering sense of self, such as that we are sinners by nature or evolved apes. We can begin to either believe that we cannot rise above this world by the power of Self or that we have no power of Self, because we are products of the material world and thus have no power over it.

THE INHERENT RISK FACTOR

The equation is simple: Descending into a physical body on earth is not without risk. There is a potential that the being who descends can become lost or trapped in a sense of self that makes it impossible for us to transcend our limitations and ascend back to the spiritual realm.

As we have said, everything in the world of form was created by spiritual beings in a higher realm. The being that you are, the being that incorporates the unique individuality that makes you you, is also created as an extension of ascended masters in the spiritual realm. Ascended masters have already gone through the process of descending into a dense sphere and then rising above any limited sense of self. Thus, they have experienced first-hand how difficult it can be, once you are inside the perception filter of an unascended sphere. Naturally, when an ascended master creates an extension of itself, it will incorporate this experience into the design.

We all realize that when we send our children to school or into adult life, they face a certain risk. If we could, we would indeed protect our children, so that nothing really bad could happen to them—we would minimize the risk. When ascended masters create extensions of themselves, they do so out of their own beings. Creating an individualized being is a very complex task, and it is a mixture of a highly scientific calculation and a work of art. So if ascended masters simply created be-

| 8 | *The Self in the spiritual realm*

ings and sent these beings into embodiment in the material world, there would be a real risk that these beings could be lost, and thus the masters would lose part of themselves.

In order to minimize the risk, the ascended masters came up with an ingenious design. When creating an individual being, they first create a self that is meant to always remain in the spiritual realm. We might call this a spiritual self, but the masters generally call it the "I AM Presence."

Your I AM Presence contains the blueprint for the highly complex and intricate design, that gives you an individuality which is different from the individuality of the other seven billion humans on earth, and different from the countless other self-aware beings inhabiting the material universe. It is even different from all of the even more innumerable lifestreams inhabiting the various levels of the spiritual realm.

Your I AM Presence contains the blueprint
for the highly complex and intricate design,
that gives you an individuality which is different
from any other individuality — completely unique.

The I AM Presence is truly a conscious being, yet it also gathers to itself energy, namely the Ma-ter light. However, the light of the I AM Presence has a higher vibration than anything found in the material universe. This means that your I AM Presence cannot in any way be affected by the energies found on earth. No matter what could possibly happen to you here on earth, none of it could affect your I AM Presence in any way. This completely eliminates the risk, that the original part of your being could be lost, changed or destroyed by anything that could happen to you here on earth.

Of course, this can be attained only because the I AM Presence is made from higher energies, and this also means, that the I AM Presence cannot descend into a physical body on a planet as dense as earth. An

The Power of Self

I AM Presence can indeed grow by remaining in the spiritual realm, as many do. Yet an I AM Presence can attain maximum growth only by making the free-will decision to send an extension of itself into the latest unascended sphere. This makes it necessary that the I AM Presence creates an extension of itself that can indeed descend, and how this occurs will be the topic of the next chapter. In the rest of this chapter, we will discuss certain characteristics of the I AM Presence. The relationship between the I AM Presence and the being that descends can be depicted as in the following image.

UNDERSTANDING YOUR HIGHER SELF

Image 8 - Your I AM Presence and your Christ Self

The I AM Presence is the inner sphere above you, surrounded by the colored rings that symbolize your causal body (explained later). The being that descends is the lower figure, and you are connected to the I AM Presence with a tube of light or crystal cord. In between the two is your Christ self (also explained later), which is a mediator, a connecting link, between your Presence and your lower being.

It is important to realize, that this image is simply one possible illustration of your Presence, and it is quite linear. It

| 8 | The Self in the spiritual realm

obviously builds on the traditional view that heaven or the spiritual realm is geographically above you.

During the Middle Ages, Christians believed that if you traveled up from the earth, you would break through a membrane and enter God's kingdom. Modern rockets have proven that to be incorrect, so it can be helpful to adopt a broader view of the Presence. Again, the following illustration is just another – and still somewhat linear – way to symbolize the relationship between you and your I AM Presence.

This image depicts the I AM presence and causal body as being right around you, meaning not separated in space. This is based on an understanding of the hierarchical structure of the world of form.

Image 9 - Being the open door for the energies from your I AM Presence

As explained earlier, the Creator created the first sphere out of its own Being, meaning God's Being is embedded in everything. After the first sphere ascended, the beings in that sphere created the second sphere out of their own beings. This process has continued until the current sphere, in which the material universe is a part. In other words, the traditional concept of a remote God high above us is simply not correct. There is a hierarchy of spiritual beings extending from the Creator through seven levels. Each level is not separated from the one above it; it is an extension of the one before it. Each new level is made from the "stuff" of the previous level, which has been lowered in vibration. There is no uncrossable barrier, simply a gradual difference in vibration.

This means there is no actual separation. Your I AM Presence is an extension of a being in the spiritual realm, and the Self that descends is an extension of your I AM Presence. Thus, you are not actually separated from your Presence. You are existing within the space, the sphere, of your Presence.

Separation is a product of your current perception filter. If you think your perception filter shows you reality, then you will identify yourself as what you see through the filter—a separate being. Yet as you transcend the perception filter (your sense of self), you will attain a state of pure awareness. You will then experience a deepening oneness with your I AM Presence, until you can say with Jesus: "I and my Father are one." At that point, you will fulfill another statement made by Jesus, namely "I am the open door, which no man can shut." You are now an open door for your I AM Presence to express itself freely in this world. As long as you still identify with your outer self, your perception filter will block (filter out) some of the flow from your Presence.

*Separation is a product of your current perception filter.
If you think your perception filter shows you reality,
then you will identify yourself as a separate being.*

The point is that you are not actually separated from your Presence, and thus there is no barrier to break down or cross. Your Presence is right here with you, and thus it is only a matter of attuning your Self to the vibrational level of your Presence.

This means there are stages in your relationship with your Presence, from lower to higher:

8 | *The Self in the spiritual realm*

Stage 1: You have no conscious connection to your Presence. You know nothing about it, or it is a theoretical concept without any inner, intuitive connection.

Stage 2: You have some connection to your Presence, but you still see it as being separated from you by a distance or a barrier. You are working on strengthening your connection, but the concept of a connection between two parts inevitably implies that the two are separated by space. At this stage, we often have intuition, mystical experiences or a sense of connection to something greater—and this is what opens us to the spiritual path. Yet our perception filters will still limit the progress we make on the path.

Stage 3: You begin to realize the need to disentangle yourself from your perception filter and attain a state of pure awareness. Thus, you start systematically questioning your perception filter, striving to see the world without looking through any filter. You begin to realize that space cannot separate you from your Presence; the sense of separation is a figment of your imagination.

Stage 4: You come to identify yourself as one with your Presence, as an extension of the Presence. This means you know you are not your lower being or body, even though you still use your body as a vehicle for expression in the material realm. You know you are not the outer personality, the ego or the separate self. You are simply the open door, a clear pane of glass.

The Power of Self

THE TWO ASPECTS OF YOUR I AM PRESENCE

One of the foundational teachings given by the ascended masters is that everything in the world of form is an expression of the one, indivisible Creator. Yet in order to create a world of differentiated forms, the one Creator first expressed itself as two complementary polarities. These can be called Yin and Yang, masculine and feminine, expanding and contracting, Alpha and Omega.

Any form that is sustainable is created from a balanced combination of the two forces. Thus, within any form created through the oneness of the spiritual hierarchy, both aspects are found. This means that your Presence also has these two basic aspects.

The name "I AM Presence" refers to the name that God gave to Moses. In most Bibles, this is translated as "I AM THAT I AM." Yet some biblical scholars are aware that a more correct translation of the original Hebrew would be "I WILL BE WHO I WILL BE." Your Presence has both aspects:

- The I AM THAT I AM is the Alpha aspect of your Presence, and it is the immutable, immovable center that connects you to the spiritual hierarchy and ultimately to the I AM THAT I AM of the Creator.

- The I WILL BE WHO I WILL BE aspect is what gives your Presence the drive to express itself in the material world. Meaning that it is out of the I WILL BE aspect that you descend.

The important point to ponder is that the I AM aspect is the immutable, never-changing center of your Presence, while the I Will Be aspect is constantly changing or rather transcending itself. This can help you realize, that you can indeed transcend any limitation in the material world or any "mistake" from your past.

The way to truly transcend is to lock in to the constant flow of the I Will Be aspect, so you do not fall prey to the lie – promoted by the ego and the false teachers of this world – that you are bound by material conditions or can never escape the mistakes you have made. It is what

| 8 | *The Self in the spiritual realm*

Jesus called the "prince of this world" that wants you – as a Spirit – to be bound by conditions or mistakes in this world. The Self that descends is an extension of the I Will Be aspect of your Presence, and once you accept that, you can indeed transcend any condition.

However, the prince of this world is a very powerful and subtle programming, that has infused the collective consciousness for a long time, and we have all been affected by it. The only way beyond it is to know that Spirit is never bound by anything in this world and will at any moment express itself as it wants to express itself.

*The I AM THAT I AM is the Alpha aspect of your
Presence, the immovable center that connects
you to the Creator.*

*The I WILL BE WHO I WILL BE aspect is what gives
your Presence the drive to express itself
in the material world.*

This is not the egoic drive to do whatever you want without facing the consequences. It is the Spirit's desire to transform the limited conditions of this world into their highest potential. And you simply cannot transform this world if you think your expression should be bound by current conditions. Thus, only when the Self becomes the open door, will you be able to truly flow with the unconditional – and thus unrestricted – creative flow of your I Will Be Presence.

You can also look at it as follows. The I AM aspect of your Presence will not change, whereas the I Will Be aspect is designed to constantly flow with the self-transcendence of life itself. Thus, the Self that descends has the free will to enter into any condition, experience or sense of identity possible on earth, but it can never be permanently bound by them. There is nothing you cannot transcend, there is no circumstance in which you can be permanently trapped. However, because the Self has free will, you can indeed believe that you are trapped by material conditions or past mistakes. And in your own mind, you will remain trapped until you again reconnect to the I Will Be aspect and decide to transcend your limitations.

The Self truly should not think or say "I am" about any condition in the material world. It is when you think "I am this lower self" that you give away your power to transcend the self and the material conditions that define it. Instead, the Self should always think in terms of "I will be." If you think "I am this limited self," your only option for escaping that self is to change it into something else. If you think, "I will be," you do not have to change the self; you simply say "I will be more than this self" or "I will now be this new self I envision." In the next chapter, we will take a closer look at the Self that descends.

CHAPTER 9

THE SELF THAT DESCENDS INTO THE MATERIAL WORLD

We have seen that the ascended masters create the I AM Presence as a repository for your unique individuality. This is done in order to ensure that your individuality could never be destroyed or distorted by what you experience in the material world. Yet we have also seen that because of this, the I AM Presence cannot itself descend into a physical body, meaning it must send an extension of itself. It is this extension which we will examine in this chapter.

Let us begin by understanding how the I AM Presence looks at the process of sending an extension of itself into embodiment. The Presence has two purposes for wanting to do this:

- It wants to grow in self-awareness.
- It wants to help raise this latest sphere, until it can ascend and become part of the spiritual realm.

How can the Presence fulfill these purposes? It has two main objectives:

- **It wants to experience the material realm from the inside.** There is an obvious difference between looking at this world as a spiritual being in a higher realm and then looking at it from the perspective of a being who is inside this world and somewhat affected by the limitations of this world. The I AM Presence wants this inside perspective, as seeing it and transcending it helps the Presence expand its sense of self.

- **The Presence wants to express its creative potential in this world.** This involves a two-fold action of expressing spiritual light through the prism of your unique individuality. It also involves bringing the spiritual perspective of the Presence as focused through your individuality. As a crude illustration, we might say that an unascended sphere has only a small amount of light, comparable to a dark room. A sphere is brought closer to the ascension point, when an I AM Presence radiates its spiritual light into the sphere. Yet this can be done only when the Presence has a focus inside the sphere and when that self sees itself as an open door for the Presence.

CREATING A SELF THAT CANNOT BE LOST

As we have seen, the above purposes can be fulfilled only by the I AM Presence creating an extension of itself and sending it into the material world. Yet we also have the concern of how this can be done so that the Self that descends cannot become permanently trapped in this world. And here is where we come to a subtle point that can be difficult to understand with the linear, analytical mind. One way to explain this is to say that the I AM Presence has two aspects:

- **Consciousness**, self-awareness or Presence. This aspect is formless.

- **Individuality**. The aspect that has form and wants to be expressed in the world of form.

As we have discussed before, some scientists are beginning to realize, that the entire universe resembles a giant mind. Mystics have long been saying that there is only one mind, namely that of the Creator, but that this one mind can express itself as many individual beings. The important point for this discussion is that the I AM Presence creates an extension of the first aspect. It creates an extension of its self-awareness, and

| 9 | *The Self that descends into the material world*

it is this extension that descends into the material universe, while the individuality remains safe and untouchable in the spiritual realm.

We can also say that self-awareness is actually beyond the world of form. It has no form, it has no characteristics that can be affected by any form. Yet individuality has form, and thus it can indeed be affected by other forms, which is how you grow in self-awareness. The point is that your individuality does not descend but remains safe in the spiritual realm. What descends in an extension of your pure self-awareness. This Self therefore has no inherent individuality; it is simply an open door for the I AM Presence.

As a crude visual illustration, consider how police teams have a flexible tube with a lens at the end, that they can insert into a room. The tube is connected to a video camera, so one can see what is happening inside the room. The I AM Presence – again only as a crude visual illustration – extends a "tube of light" into the material universe, and at the end of it is a clear, glass lens. The lens works both ways. The I AM Presence can send light into the material world through the lens, and it can experience the material world from the inside by looking through the lens. The lens itself is simply pure awareness, and as such it can never be lost in or distorted by anything it encounters in the material world. Yet the lens can be expanded, and this is what happens as you grow towards higher states of consciousness. You become both an open door and a wider door.

KNOWING THROUGH A MYSTICAL EXPERIENCE: GNOSIS

The ascended masters realize that you can know the reality of this teaching only if you have what we earlier called mystical experiences. Normally, the mind of a human being is completely focused on or absorbed in concrete thoughts, thoughts that have some kind of form. The thoughts can be compared to the contents of a container, but then what is the container itself? The container is consciousness in its pure form. What the mystics of all ages have said is that if we can still the mind, if we can get beyond being so absorbed in thoughts, it is possible to have an experience of consciousness in its pure form. The philosopher René Descartes is famous for saying: "I think, therefore I am." A mystic might take that statement one step further and say: "Yes, but what is it that enables you to think? It is that you have Presence, self-awareness." Thus, we might also say: "I AM, therefore I have self-awareness which enables me to think."

The ascended masters are quite aware that for many people, this concept of a Self that has no individuality or form will be contrary to everything they were brought up to believe. And thus, such people might indeed argue for or against this Self by using the analytical mind. Yet the masters also teach that the analytical mind has certain limitations, namely that it can only deal with something that has form.

It is precisely this characteristic of the analytical mind, that makes it possible for us to believe that we are material beings who cannot transcend certain limitations. The analytical mind must compare everything to something that is known in its own database. But how can you transcend what is known by using what is known? As Albert Einstein put it: "You cannot solve a problem with the same state of consciousness that created the problem."

As we will later discuss in more detail, it is possible for us to create a self that is defined based on the limitations of the material world. Once the Self that descends begins to identify itself with such a separate self, everything it sees will be colored by limitations, and thus it will seemingly confirm these limitations. This is another way to describe the human dilemma, the existential catch-22.

There is only one way out, namely to have a direct experience, which shows you that you are more than this worldly, separate self. And this will happen only when you experience that you are beyond your normal thoughts, while still remaining conscious and alive. You are conscious without being conscious of or identified with your normal sense of self. It is precisely this mystical experience that becomes the foundation for starting the process, whereby you gradually dis-identify yourself from the separate self. Thus, the Self that descended can return to its original

| 9 | *The Self that descends into the material world*

state, in which it realizes it is an open door for the I AM Presence—nothing more, nothing less.

Many spiritual people have already had such mystical experiences, and you might be one of them. Have you ever had the sense that you were connected to something greater, that you were one with a greater reality, perhaps everything or even God? Have you ever experienced being conscious without being aware of your environment or the thoughts that normally fill your head? Have you ever had visions of a world or level of reality beyond the material world? Have you ever had a sense that "you" are much bigger than your body or that you are like a cell in a larger body? There are many types of these mystical experiences, and they come in various degrees of purity. Yet the important point is that any experience that is beyond what we call "normal" human awareness, shows you that the core of your being, the Self that descended, is truly a form of pure awareness.

When your mind is purified from misqualified energies, you will naturally and effortlessly start having mystical experiences.

If you have not had such experiences, do not despair. As we have already discussed, the ascended masters have given us many tools for helping us have experiences of a higher state of consciousness. When you purify the four levels of your mind from misqualified energies, you will naturally and effortlessly start having mystical experiences. The reason is that for the Self that descends, pure awareness is its natural state.

The important point to ponder is that the Self that descends is pure awareness, meaning it has no form. As such it cannot be destroyed or killed by anything in the material world. It cannot be permanently trapped in or confined to any form. And no matter what sense of self you might have right now, the pure Self that you truly are has the potential to transcend every aspect of it. No matter what you have experienced or are experiencing, you have the potential to remake your sense of self, so you become an open door, whereby your true spiritual individuality can be expressed freely through the lens of the Self that is in this world.

This, of course, leaves the question of how you came to forget that you are a spiritual being, and we will discuss that in the rest of this chapter. However, let us first give a more practical name to "the Self that descends." Although many names can be used, the ascended masters have chosen the name: "Conscious You," to signify that this is the Self that makes it possible for you to be ultimately conscious or aware. You attain this when you are aware that you are indeed the I Will Be Presence while still being aware of the material world and your potential for co-creating a higher form in this world.

HOW DOES THE SELF EXPRESS ITSELF?

Once again, the Conscious You is created in order to minimize the risk that it could get lost in this world. And once again, this means that because of the rather large difference in vibration between the spiritual realm and the material world, the Conscious You cannot interact directly with a physical body. In order to actually take embodiment, the Conscious You starts by projecting itself into a sense of self that is made from the energies and forms currently found on earth. And then this self can interact with the physical body.

The wisdom of this design is that even if the material self was damaged or destroyed, nothing would happen to the Conscious You. The lower energies of the material world simply cannot affect the pure self-awareness of the Conscious You. This is not so difficult to visualize, when you accept reincarnation. You know that the soul is not destroyed when the physical body dies. And likewise the Conscious You is not destroyed if the outer self dies.

The process of how we took embodiment is complex, and we will here look at a condensed version. In the original design, we would start by descending into a protected environment in what we earlier called the

| 9 | *The Self that descends into the material world*

identity realm, which is the highest of the four realms of the material universe. We would spend some time in a spiritual learning environment, called a mystery school.

Here we would start by learning how to take on and transcend a material self without identifying with it. As long as we do not identify with a material self, we can transcend that self, and it is this process of taking on and transcending a self that causes us to grow in self-awareness. As we gained more experience, we could even begin to define our own selves, and this would then become the basis for us descending into a physical body.

Again, there is a substantial difference in the vibration of the identity realm and the material realm. The material realm is much more dense, so the moment we do descend into a physical body, our perspective changes dramatically. The human body is obviously very much limited by material conditions, which means that if we identify with the body, it will seem very believable that material conditions have power over us.

WHY HAS THE SELF FORGOTTEN WHO IT IS?

What we now see is that in order to descend into the density of the material world, the Conscious You takes on a self made from the forms and energies of the material world. This self is like a perception filter, that we might compare to a pair of colored glasses. Consider what would happen if someone had put red contact lenses in front of your eyes when you were born. You would have grown up being firmly convinced that the sky really is purple and that there is no other way to experience the sky.

We now see that what gives external conditions power over us is the belief that what we see through the filter is a reality, which is independent of our perception. This is what we earlier illustrated by comparing the mind to a kaleidoscope. The colored glass pieces in the kaleidoscope correspond to the many beliefs you have in your mind, and these beliefs make it seem believable, that you are a limited being and that the material world has power over you.

The Power of Self

Once you begin to realize that the way you look at life may be a product of a particular kind of self, a particular perception filter, a tantalizing opportunity opens up. We can now ask a potentially life-changing question: "Is my current self the only way I could possibly look at the world, or is there a different way—a way that would help me transcend my current limitations?"

The central problem in human existence:
We experience life through a perception filter, but fail to
see that this is just one among many possible filters.

Obviously, we can all see that there are many other people who don't look at life the way we do. The logical explanation is that they are experiencing the world through a variety of different selves, different perception filters. This idea explains why it can be so difficult to agree with others, or even communicate with them. If you have a person wearing yellow glasses and a person wearing red glasses, they will not be able to agree on the color of the sky, because they each see something different.

So what do we do now? Well, we can engage in a process of refining or expanding our perception filters by increasing our understanding of life and spiritual topics. This is what many of us have done by studying spiritual or self-help teachings. We gain a deeper understanding of the spiritual aspects of life, and it does help us shift our perception of life.

Yet, we can see that this approach has some limitations. For example, many spiritual people still have certain character traits or habits that they cannot transcend. In fact, some people have even used a spiritual teaching to build a new perception filter, that in many ways limits them as much as the filters they had before finding a spiritual teaching. Some spiritual people are engaged in the struggle to convince other people that: "My perception filter is right and yours is wrong," a struggle that has been going on for a long time on this planet. Some even have a sense

9 | The Self that descends into the material world

of superiority, because they feel their spiritual guru or teaching gives them a perception that is superior to all others.

This is not to say that studying a spiritual teaching is wrong or that it is wrong to expand your perception filter. Yet the ascended masters say that this is only a phase, and there is an even higher level of the spiritual path. What might the next level be?

Well, how about we ask another question: "Is it possible to experience life without *any* perception filter at all?" In other words, is it possible to transcend all perception filters instead of merely expanding them? And as we have already seen, the Conscious You is truly created to be an open door for the I AM Presence. Being an open door means that you have no perception filter; it means that you do not see the material world through any filter created from the energies and forms found in this world. Instead, you see the material world as your I AM Presence sees it; you see with pure perception.

This is a concept found in many mystical teachings. For example, the founder of Tibetan Buddhism, PadmaSambhava, called it "pure awareness" or "naked awareness." Zen Buddhism calls it "beginner's mind" and Jesus talked about us becoming as little children in order to enter the kingdom of heaven. When you see the world with pure perception, you also see that everything in this world is made from a lower form of energy than what streams from your I AM Presence. Thus, you will literally experience that "with God all things are possible." Energy is simply made from waves, and a wave of a lower vibration can be changed by interacting with a wave of a higher vibration. Thus, for those who are open doors for spiritual energy, all things are indeed possible.

QUESTIONING THE PERCEPTION FILTER

We can now see that the concept of spiritual growth that leads to a higher state of consciousness is truly a process, whereby we take off the perception filters we have taken on. As long as you look at life through the perception filter that defines your current sense of self, there is absolutely no way you can question the belief that material conditions are real and have power over you. The *only* way you might transcend these conditions is to question the very perception filter that makes them seem real. Yet you cannot do this as long as you look at life from inside the perception filter. This is what we earlier called the human enigma, the existential catch-22. The Conscious You cannot question its perception, as long as it is looking at itself through the perception filter of the material self.

*Being an open door means that
you have no perception filter.
You see the material world
as your I AM Presence sees it.*

The only way out is a mystical experience, whereby you realize that you are *not* your current sense of self. In reality, you are a being that descended from the spiritual realm, and as such you cannot be permanently affected by anything on earth. This being has simply taken on a limited self, and as long as you see yourself through the filter of that self, you think this is who you are. Yet regardless of your current perception, you are still the same being that descended.

As a visual illustration, imagine that someone has given you a pair of binoculars. As long as you are looking through them, you can indeed see certain things more clearly than with the naked eye. Yet the price you pay is that the binoculars give you a very narrow field of view. So in order to get back to a fuller perspective, you simply have to pull your eyes away from the binoculars and see the world with the "naked eye." Likewise, you can gradually learn to pull the Conscious You away from the binoculars of the outer self.

The next step is to consider how the Conscious You took on your current self. It did so by projecting itself into that self, much like an actor who puts on a certain costume and make-up in order to play a role in a theater performance or movie. Your current self is simply a role that you

| 9 | *The Self that descends into the material world*

have chosen to play in the theater of life. Yet if you are beginning to have had enough of playing this part, you can begin to take off the costume.

How do you transcend your current self? By realizing that the Conscious You projected itself into this self, which means it also has the potential to pull itself back out. The way to do this is to realize, that the Conscious You has the potential to attain the state of pure awareness, meaning you have *no* perception filter. You simply look at conditions in the material realm without labeling or judging them. The labeling and judging is a product of your perception filter.

Once you see that your outer self is just a perception filter and that nothing you see through it is ultimately real, it becomes easier for you to stop identifying with it. In fact, once you have had an experience of pure awareness, you can never again be fully identified with your outer self, although it may still take some time to completely overcome the sense of identification.

It is essential to realize that the Conscious You has not been permanently changed by your current sense of self—any more than your eyes would be changed if you put on a pair of yellow glasses. The Conscious You is perfectly capable of attaining a state of pure awareness, where you do not have any of the perception filters defined on earth. You see things as they really are.

This is what Jesus talked about when he said: "When thine eye be single, thy whole body shall be full of light." Think about that statement. When your vision is "single," meaning it is not divided by any perception filters, then you see that everything in the material universe is made from spiritual light. How does this help you transcend your limitations?

DISMANTLING THE PERCEPTION FILTERS

As explained earlier, everything in the material universe is made from spiritual light that has simply taken on a temporary appearance. Yet as long as you are looking at the world through the perception filter of a material self, these temporary appearances will seem real.

This is an important principle to understand. Our perception filter has no actual power over us; yet it can take away our power, because we have no frame of reference from outside the filter. Why did medieval people believe in the infallibility of the Catholic doctrine that the earth was the center of the universe? Because they did not have the frame of reference provided by early astronomers, who said: "Excuse me, but the objects in the sky don't actually behave according to doctrine, so why should we?"

When your vision is "single," meaning it is not divided by any perception filters, then you see that everything in the material universe is made from spiritual light.

Once again, let us look at the example of a maze made out of tall hedges. Entering the maze is like taking on a perception filter, because all you see is green walls and you have no awareness of what the maze looks like from above. You have no way of knowing your position relative to the exit.

So what do you do? Well, you can bumble around and hope to run into the exit by sheer luck. Or you can use the mind's ability to mentally step outside your situation, whereby you observe your movements and try to imagine a map of the maze based on what you see around you. Yet a third option is to notice that there are ropes hanging down from above, and if you climb such a rope, you can see the maze from above. Climbing the rope is using the Conscious You's ability to mentally step outside your current perception filter.

The principle is simple. Our perception blinds us to reality; it presents us with a distorted or erroneous view of reality. Yet as long as we look through the filter, there is no way we can see how our view is distorted. In order to free ourselves from our perception filter, we need a frame of reference that shows us there is a reality outside the filter.

| 9 | *The Self that descends into the material world*

If you look at history, you will see that all religions were meant to provide us with a frame of reference from outside our perception filter. Both Jesus and the Buddha sought to challenge our self-image as powerless beings. Unfortunately, we humans have an ability to use religion as a way to validate our current perception, and that is why so many religions have actually trapped people even more firmly in the belief that we are powerless human beings who need someone from outside ourselves.

Our perception blinds us to reality;
it presents us with a distorted view of reality.
Yet as long as we look through the filter,
there is no way we can see how our view is distorted.

In medieval times, people were very firmly trapped in the perception filter created by the Catholic Church. Science became the frame of reference for showing people that there was a reality outside doctrine. And science still functions as such, but materialism has limited the liberating power of science. Which is why so many people in today's age are turning to spirituality or mysticism, which recognizes the inbuilt power of our minds. What is that power?

Well, when we take the concept of the Conscious You, the real power is that you are a spiritual being who has projected itself into your current self. And the very ability that allowed you to project yourself into your current perception filter can also be used to project yourself outside your current perception filter. We earlier said that the only way to know whether the ascended masters are real is to have a direct, mystical experience. Such an experience is the product of the Conscious You projecting itself outside your current perception filter.

As said before, mystical experiences are a direct demonstration of the fact that the Conscious You is more than your current self. They come when the Conscious You stops being fully identified with the outer self and instead experiences a glimpse of what it truly is. As you walk the spiritual path, you will start having more of such experiences, and they will become gradually more clear. Eventually, you can start having experiences of a state of pure awareness, where you have no thoughts or value judgments. You simply experience the world without any perception filter. And such an experience is the ultimate proof that what the Conscious You has projected itself into, could never permanently affect the Self.

This is when you will begin to believe the central message of the ascended masters: What the Self has gotten itself into, it can also get itself out of. And this is not a matter of finding an outer savior who will do all the work for you. It is simply a matter of making conscious use of the very same abilities that allowed you to get into your current sense of self. The ascended masters have never promised that they will save us, or even do something for us. What they will do is to help us discover the power that has always been available to us: the power of Self. This power is obviously being blocked by the perception filter which says that material conditions have power over us. So by transcending such perception filters, we become the open doors for the full power of our higher selves.

HOW WE CREATE A LIMITED SELF HERE ON EARTH

As we are all aware, planet earth currently has many manifestations that are not the highest possible. Man's inhumanity to man is truly one of the conditions that we all have to grapple with. The result is that after we first took embodiment, we were all affected by the impure conditions on this planet, and most of us therefore started creating a new self in response to the conditions we experienced. This self was obviously based on the much more limited perception we had after we took embodiment. In fact, in many cases we simply took on a predefined self in order to cope with the conditions on earth.

Compare this to a theater. Imagine a new actor, who is pushed onto an empty stage in the middle of a gala performance and told he has to

| 9 | *The Self that descends into the material world*

come up with his own role. This would obviously be very scary, so a new actor would likely prefer to take on a small role and hide behind a costume and make-up. As the actor gradually grows in confidence, he or she can take on more complex roles. And in some cases, an actor can even gather the courage to walk on stage without playing a predefined role.

As the Conscious You first descended into embodiment, you took on one of the many predefined roles that are available in the theater of earth. Yet the earth is currently in a much lower state than when it was created by ascended beings. Almost every religious and spiritual teaching contains the concept that in the past, there was a higher state, and we humans have descended or fallen below it. As a result, there are now many predefined roles that were not available in the original design.

The ascended masters teach that this "fall" happened because a number of people chose to create or take on selves based on the illusion of separation. This makes it possible that you can act as a separate being without considering what consequences your actions have for other people, for the whole or for yourself in the long term. Currently, most people on earth are acting from such a separate self, and that is why there is so much conflict. There are two main reasons why people take on a separate self:

- In the past, you decided that you wanted to experience the world through a limited self or that you wanted to do the kind of things that can only be done when you think you are a separate being. And while this is perfectly allowed by the Law of Free Will, the simple fact is that once you take on a role based on the illusion of separation, you forget that you are a Conscious You that is an extension of the I AM Presence. And that means the perception filter of a separate self seems far more real than the perception of a connected being.

- It is possible that you did not descend because you wanted to act as a separate being. You might have taken on a limited self in order to demonstrate to others, that we are more than human beings and that we do not have to be limited by material conditions. Instead, we can rise above any sense of self and help co-create a new world that is beyond current limitations.

Whatever the reason you had for taking on a separate self, the teachings of the ascended masters offer you a way to rise above your current perception filter and attain the state of pure awareness that is your highest potential. Then, you can fulfill your reason for being, namely to be an open door for your I AM Presence.

We can now see what is the biggest challenge on the spiritual path. It is to let go of all our pre-conceived opinions and beliefs—let go of our perception filters. So many of us go through a phase, where we think we have found a true spiritual teaching, and now we don't need to transcend certain beliefs, because they will surely be validated when we enter heaven. Yet any teaching expressed in words is less than the spiritual reality. Thus, the real challenge is to let go of everything—especially what we believe we do not need to question.

It is not by holding on to anything – clutching your ideas, as the Buddhists say – that you will get to the ascended state. It is only by letting go of every "thing" and attaining the state of pure, naked awareness in which you have no human value judgments, no judgments after appearances. It is only when you do not judge after earthly appearances, that the current appearances on earth will have no power over you.

CHAPTER 10

THE "SELF" THAT IS CREATED IN THE MATERIAL WORLD

There are certain words that are used by different people to mean so many different things, that the words almost become useless. One example is the word "soul." It has been used for centuries by different religious and spiritual teachings to mean many different things. And it is often used without clearly defining it, based on the assumption that people know what it means. The ascended masters offer us a more nuanced understanding by breaking the soul, or the lower being, into different components.

As mentioned before, many spiritual people accept the concept of reincarnation, and it is commonly assumed, that it is the soul that reincarnates. This also leads to the common assumption that the soul was created in a higher realm and then descended into the material realm. Which means it is the soul that ascends back to the spiritual realm. This then leads to two common ideas about what you need to do in order to get your soul to qualify for entry into the spiritual realm:

- The soul has "fallen" or descended into a lower state, so it no longer qualifies for heaven. Thus, you need to compensate for the errors you have made and purify or raise the soul.

- The soul is meant to be perfected, thus it is your task to raise your soul to a state of perfection (however it is defined).

What can revolutionize your understanding of the soul is the concept of the Conscious You. The core understanding is that it was the Conscious You that originally descended and started the process of you being in embodiment in the material world. Thus, it is the Conscious You that has the potential to ascend back to the spiritual realm.

Yet this ascension process does *not* happen by the Conscious You compensating for an imperfect state or seeking to attain a state of perfection based on earthly or man-made criteria. On the contrary, the Conscious You can ascend *only* by fulfilling its highest potential, which is to be in a state of pure awareness, where it can function as an open door for the Presence. This has two aspects:

- The I AM Presence can express itself through the open door of the Conscious You, by letting its light and individuality flow into the material realm.

- The Presence can experience the material world through the Conscious You, which is a clear pane of glass with no perception filter.

In other words, in its highest state, the Conscious You does not have a sense of self as a separate being. It sees itself as nothing more and nothing less than an open door for the Presence to express itself in this world and as a clear pane of glass for the Presence to experience this world. The Conscious You in this state sees itself as the I Will Be aspect of the I AM Presence.

The Conscious You in its highest state has no perception filter. Thus, it does not block or hold back any expression coming from the Presence, and it does not block anything it experiences from reaching the Presence. The Conscious You does not judge after appearances, but allows the Presence to evaluate its experiences, and then learn from them, storing the results in the causal body (explained later). Compare this to how often we evaluate our intuitive insights, in order to see whether they are appropriate according to an earthly standard. Then consider how often we seek to hide something from God.

10 | The Self that is created in the material world

It is now important to understand, that the Conscious You did not originally descend in a state of pure awareness. Let us look at why.

HOW THE CONSCIOUS YOU DESCENDED

The material world is created from spiritual light that was reduced in vibration by the reduction factors represented by the seven rays. This means that the material world was originally at a certain level of vibration, meaning it was made from energies that had a greater density than the spiritual realm. This accounts for the fact, that we do not perceive the spiritual realm through our physical senses. The senses are attuned to the vibrations in the material frequency spectrum, and these vibrations are currently so much lower than the spiritual vibrations, that our senses cannot bridge the gap and "see" the spiritual realm (many spiritual people can sense and experience spiritual energies intuitively, but generally not through the physical senses).

The Conscious You is created with a point-like sense of self, which it has the potential to raise through many levels, until it attains the same omni-present sense of self as the Creator.

The purpose of creating the material realm with a higher density is to facilitate the growth of self-aware beings—us. By descending into a realm where there is no direct perception of the spiritual world, we have the opportunity to gradually raise our consciousness, until we can serve as an open door between the spiritual and the material realm. By going through this process, we also help to raise the vibrations of the material realm, until it vibrates at the level of the spiritual realm.

The Power of Self

For the purpose of the present discussion, the important point is that the Conscious You does not descend with its highest self-awareness. The Conscious You is created with a point-like sense of self, which it has the potential to raise or expand through many levels, until it attains the same omni-present sense of self as the Creator. Take note of what is being said. The task of the Conscious You is *not* to build a perfect self in this world. The task of the Conscious You is to expand its sphere of awareness. Yet it does this by taking on a limited self and then transcending that self by realizing: "I am more than that self." Every time the Conscious You goes through this forgetting and awakening, it broadens the sphere of its awareness.

In order to descend into the denser vibrations of the material universe, the Conscious You needs a vehicle, meaning a sense of self that is made from the same vibrations as the material realm. Here is the important realization: the Conscious You takes on this vehicle; it does *not* become the vehicle. The Conscious You is *not* changed by this process; it is only its sense of self – its perception – that is changed. Again, it is like an actor who puts on a costume and makeup in order to play a role in a theater performance—meaning that the actor can take off the costume as easily as it is put on.

Originally, the Conscious You descended into a sense of self that was made from the same basic vibrations out of which the material universe was created. It is this self, this vehicle, that we – from a higher perspective – can call the soul.

Yet take note that this soul was *not* created in the spiritual realm, nor was it created from the vibrations of the spiritual realm. It was, as Genesis says, created from dust, meaning material energies. Thus, the soul – according to this definition – did not descend from the spiritual realm and consequently cannot ascend. It is the Conscious You that can ascend, but only when it stops identifying itself with or as the soul and instead attains its highest potential—the state of pure awareness in which it sees itself as one with the Presence.

Take note of one potential point of confusion. The soul does descend into the physical body when you take embodiment, and in many cases it does come from a higher realm. That is because your soul vehicle survives the death of the physical body and the Conscious You carries the soul over to its next embodiment. Depending on your level of consciousness, the soul vehicle may indeed rise to a higher level of the material world between embodiments – we earlier mentioned the four levels – and then descend from there into the next embodiment. However, these levels are not the spiritual realm, so the soul still cannot ascend and become a spiritual being.

WHY THE SOUL CANNOT ASCEND

There is a subtle distinction to be made. The soul has what most people call individuality or personality. Yet this was created based on the conditions found in the material universe when the Conscious You first descended. The personality and individuality you have today is a product of the experiences you have had during your sojourn in the material world. Many elements have likely been added to the original soul into which the Conscious You descended.

Image 10 - The soul filled with dense energies

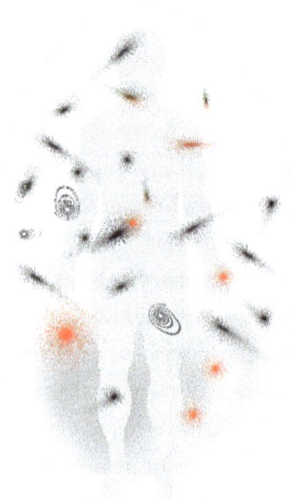

Yet all of this outer personality and individuality is *not* who you are. You truly are the individuality anchored in your I AM Presence. This individuality can potentially be expressed through the Conscious You, but the outer personality, that you have created as a reaction to conditions in the material world, will block or color this expression.

In order to ascend, it is *not* a matter of perfecting the outer personality; it is a matter of transcending it. The soul is created from certain beliefs, and they qualify the spiritual energies with a lower vibration. We might say that the ideas or beliefs that define your soul create a matrix or mesh, and the energies you qualify through those beliefs fill up the "cage" with greater and greater density. The more dense the energies become, the more the Conscious You will identify itself with the soul, and the more difficult it will be for you to extricate yourself from this identification. You simply cannot see anything beyond the energies and beliefs of the soul, because the energies form a magnetic pull that draws your attention into focusing on the lower self.

The key to spiritual growth is to begin to raise the vibration of the energies stored in your soul. As the density becomes less, the Conscious You will begin to have glimpses of a higher state of awareness. First, they will be intuitive flashes or a sense that there must be more to life. Then there will be a sense of being connected to something greater. And finally, you will begin to have glimpses of pure awareness, where you directly experience that the Conscious You is *more* than your lower individuality.

The Conscious You needs a vehicle – the soul – meaning a sense of self that is made from the same vibrations as the material realm, into which it descends.

This is when you can begin to seriously question the beliefs that make up your soul, gradually raising your sense of self, until you attain a sense of oneness with your Presence. In the process of doing this, you will also help raise the vibration of the material universe and you will help question the beliefs in the mass consciousness, making it easier for other people to raise their consciousness. Eventually, as enough people do this, the entire planet will be raised to a higher level, where it becomes obvious to most people that life has a spiritual side.

Yet, let us return to the central idea here. The outer personality and individuality – the outer self – that you currently have was created over

| 10 | *The Self that is created in the material world*

many lifetimes as a reaction to the imperfect conditions in the material world. Thus, it can *never* be perfected so that it can ascend to the spiritual realm. What can ascend is the Conscious You, the Self that first descended. Yet the Conscious You can ascend only by coming to dis-identify itself from the outer self.

It does so by transcending the limiting beliefs and raising the energies that make up the soul. Thus, in a sense one can say that the soul is raised, but it is not raised as a separate self. The limiting beliefs are dissolved and the lower energies are accelerated to a higher vibration. If you put a pot of water on the stove and let it boil until all the water is gone, would you say the pot of water was raised into a higher realm? No, obviously it was the water that was raised and the pot is left.

The point being that most of us have been tricked into following an outer path, where we seek to use a spiritual teaching to perfect the soul according to some standard. Yet the soul can never be perfected; it must be allowed to die gradually. Saint Paul said; "I die daily," meaning that a bit of his soul died as he let go of limiting beliefs. Jesus allowed himself to be crucified in order to illustrate that the Conscious You is crucified (paralyzed) by its identification with the outer self or soul. The last act of Jesus on the cross was to "give up the ghost," which was a symbol for the last remnant of his soul/outer self.

The key to spiritual growth is to begin to raise the vibration of the energies stored in your soul. As the density becomes less, the Conscious You will begin to have glimpses of a higher state of awareness.

So as Jesus said: "No man can ascend back to heaven, save he that descended from heaven." And the "man" that descended was the Conscious You, which ascends by becoming aware of its true identity—as the I Will Be aspect of the I AM Presence. In other words, the "soul" is *not* what originally took embodiment. It is something that has been created and added on to over many lifetimes. Thus, what reincarnates is both the Conscious You and the soul. Yet what originally incarnated was the Conscious You only.

On the following pages, we will look at some of the other aspects of your lower being, some of which are part of your soul.

THE CONTAINER OF SELF AND YOUR FOUR LOWER BODIES

Some mystical teachings associate Spirit or the spiritual realm with a circle as a symbol for oneness. They associate the material realm with a square. Thus, the material realm is created by "squaring the circle." Other mystical teachings relate the square to the base of the pyramid. Thus, by mastering the four elements of the material realm, you gradually rise higher, until you reach the apex of the pyramid, which is a singularity that forms the doorway between the spiritual realm and the material realm. This corresponds to the nexus of the figure-eight in the following image, and as you rise on the spiritual path, the Conscious You finds its rightful place at the apex of the pyramid of self.

Image 11 - The Conscious You in the nexus of the figure-eight flow between the spiritual and material realm

The four sides of the square or the four elements, correspond to what we mentioned earlier, namely that the material universe has four realms or octaves. Your lower self – the vehicle through which the Conscious

10 | *The Self that is created in the material world*

You expresses itself in the material world – also has four "bodies" or four levels of the mind. These are interpenetrating energy bodies that co-exist in the same space because they vibrate at different levels of frequencies. They are:

• **The identity body**, also called the etheric body. The contents of your identity body define your sense of identity. How do you see yourself, how do you see God, how do you see the world and how do you see the interaction between them? Do you see yourself as a spiritual being who is here to take dominion over the earth, and thus has the power to accomplish this? Or do you see yourself as a material being, a product of the earth with limited power to change your circumstances?

• **The mental body** contains your thoughts. It is here you form a mental image of the specific things you want to do in the material world and how to accomplish them. This mental image will be based upon your sense of identity, which defines parameters for what you think you can or cannot do. Thus, if you identify yourself as a human being, you will limit what you think you can do.

• **The emotional body** is obviously the seat of your feelings. Emotion means Energy in **MOTION**. Your thoughts are mental images, but in order to become actions or manifest forms, they must be set in motion, and this happens at the level of the emotional body. However, this body also contains your desires, and they can conflict with your higher goals. Ideally, your emotions should be reflections of your thoughts, that are reflections of your sense of identity, that again is a reflection of your Divine individuality. Yet it is common that the emotions take on a life of their own and seek to run your life, instead of being controlled by your thoughts.

• **The physical brain and the "body mind."** Many materialistic scientists believe all of our thoughts and feelings are products of the physical brain. And while this is not correct, it is indeed correct that the physical brain is a very complex "computer," that is fully capable of producing many of our thoughts and sensations. However, the physical brain is only the hardware for a level of the mind that the ascended masters call the body mind. This is the mind that is in charge of taking care of the needs of the physical body, such as the need for protection, food and propagation.

The essential question now becomes: which of your four lower bodies is your conscious mind centered upon?

For a large percentage of humankind, their conscious awareness is centered on the physical body and the material world. This means that many of their thoughts and feelings are products of the physical brain and body mind. For example, many people focus most of their attention on the basic bodily needs of protection, food, clothing and sex.

Most spiritual people have expanded their conscious awareness to encompass at least parts of the three higher bodies. Continuing to expand this conscious awareness is the key to attaining mastery over your four lower bodies, so they become vehicles that support your spiritual mission in this wold.

HOW YOU LOST CONTACT WITH YOUR SPIRITUAL SELF

The essential concept is that your four lower bodies form a filter that colors the light streaming from your I AM Presence into your lower being. Everything is energy, everything is created from the Ma-ter Light. What keeps you alive and gives you the ability to act in the material world is a stream of energy, that flows from your I AM Presence into your four lower bodies.

Ideally, you should qualify this energy with a high vibration – raising up yourself and all life – which will allow it to flow back up to your spiritual self. It will then be multiplied and you receive more energy in return, which increases your creative powers. This turns your life into an upward spiral, that empowers you to fulfill your reason for being and take dominion over your material circumstances.

This flow of energy can be compared to the light coming from the light bulb in a movie projector. As this light passes through your four

| 10 | *The Self that is created in the material world*

lower bodies, it is colored by the contents (images, beliefs and energy) of those bodies. It is like the light in a movie projector that is colored by the images on the film strip—only you have four film strips.

If you have beliefs and images in your four lower bodies that are out of harmony with your own higher Being – especially when you have self-centered beliefs and selfish desires – you will impose imperfect images upon the spiritual light. This will lead to unbalanced actions that produce suffering in your life, and it is possible to create a downward spiral that leads to more and more suffering.

What keeps you alive and gives you the ability to act in the material world is a stream of energy, that flows from your I AM Presence into your four lower bodies.

Imposing imperfect images upon the Ma-ter light will produce energy of a lower vibration. This misqualified energy cannot flow back up to your spiritual self and become your treasure laid up in heaven—it cannot enter the higher vibrations of the spiritual realm. Thus, selfish actions break the figure-eight flow and the misqualified energy has to go somewhere. The misqualified energy you produce will stay at that level of vibration indefinitely. The energy will not simply disappear but will be stored in your four lower bodies.

This energy will form a filter or veil – EVIL means Energy **VEIL** – that prevents you from maintaining contact with your spiritual self. This can gradually cloud your vision, until you think you are a human being confined to the material universe with nothing beyond it. It also reduces your creative powers, until you think your only option for doing anything on earth is to use your physical body. The accumulated energy has robbed you of your mental powers.

Take note that misqualified energies will accumulate in your four lower bodies. And the more energy that is accumulated in a particular body, the more it will pull your conscious attention into focusing on that body. Thus, many people have so much misqualified energy at the physical level, that their attention is literally imprisoned in the physical body. Other people live their lives through their emotions, while still others spend an entire lifetime being focused on the intellectual mind.

When you understand that what occurs at the conscious level – including your outer circumstances – is simply an image projected upon the screen of your mind and the Ma-ter light, you realize that in order to change what is projected onto the screen of life, you have to go to the projection room and change the film strips in your four lower bodies. Life at the conscious level can be compared to the level of the movie screen. If you don't like the movie that is playing in the theater, how much can you change the movie by working at the level of the screen? You are much more likely to be successful, when you go to the source and change the images on the film strip, meaning the contents of your four lower bodies.

When you understand this dynamic, it becomes very obvious that there are two key elements for making progress on the spiritual path:

- Purify all levels of your mind – your four lower "bodies" – from the imperfect beliefs that cause you to misqualify spiritual energy and respond to life with limiting beliefs and feelings.

- Purify – transform – the misqualified energy stored in your four lower bodies. You must lighten your load before you start climbing a mountain.

That is why it is so important to use the decrees and invocations to invoke spiritual light, that can transform the energies in your four lower bodies. Only by lessening the pull, can you free your conscious attention to focus on one of your higher bodies. Only by purifying all of your four lower bodies, will you free your attention to focus on the I AM Presence. As mentioned, I have personally used decrees for a long time, and I have felt that they provided me with a steady force that propelled me forward on the spiritual path. I am not thereby saying that decrees alone will give you progress, because you obviously also need to examine your limiting beliefs. Yet the decrees are like the motor in the vehicle, and by giving

| 10 | *The Self that is created in the material world*

them you provide the forward motion. It is then up to you to direct the vehicle, so it goes where you want it to go.

CHAPTER 11

ESCAPING THE PRISON OF THE EGO

As is the case with the word "soul," the word "ego" has been used differently by various spiritual teachings, psychologists and self-help experts. And truly, it is difficult to define the ego, because the primary effect of the ego is that it distorts your vision. Thus, as you walk the spiritual path, you will have to deal with different manifestations of the ego.

The ascended masters explain that there are 144 levels of consciousness possible on earth. We will later talk more about this, but for now the important point is that when the Conscious You first descended into embodiment on earth, it descended at the 48th level. It then had the option to start an upward spiral, whereby it would rise from the 48th level, through the succeeding levels, until it reached the 144th level and could ascend.

On each level of consciousness, there is a corresponding aspect of the ego. It is this ego that makes a particular level of consciousness seem real and seem like it has some power to hold the Conscious You at that level. In other words, the ego will seek to make the Self believe that it cannot, is not allowed to, or does not need to rise beyond its current level. Thus, in order to rise from one level of consciousness to the next, the Conscious You will have to transcend the corresponding aspect of the ego.

While this may sound difficult, it really isn't so hard, once you begin to intuitively "see" how the ego works. The ego only has a limited number of options, and some "tricks" are reused at each level of conscious-

| 11 | *Escaping the prison of the ego*

ness, so you can learn to recognize them. The primary trick used by the ego is to divert your attention away from looking inside yourself.

Jesus made an interesting statement, when he asked us why we so often look at the splinter in the eyes of our brothers but fail to see the beam in our own eyes. The primary reason for this is that the ego is so good at diverting our attention by making us believe that we have to do something, solve some problem or pay attention to something outside ourselves. The basic key to rising from one level of consciousness to the next is to look inside ourselves and realize two things:

- My current level of consciousness is limiting me, and I no longer want to be at this level.

- I, meaning the Conscious You, am more than my current level of consciousness, meaning that I can extricate myself from my current sense of self and rise – or be reborn – into a new sense of self.

Yet in order for you to come to the point of being willing to leave the old self behind, you need to see it for what it is. And you simply cannot do that as long as you are looking outside yourself, seeking to change other people or the world according to the perception you have at your current level of consciousness.

As explained before, your current level of consciousness forms a perception filter. As long as you are looking at the world through that filter, you will see the world a certain way, and your ego will seek to make you believe, that what you see is ultimate reality, absolute truth or the only way to look at life. Meaning that your current perception is something you cannot question, something you are not allowed to question or do not need to question.

Compare this to a chess game, where the rules have been altered in such a way, that no move you make will make your opponent checkmate. In other words, no matter what you do, you cannot win the game. You will either play the game indefinitely, or you will come to a point, where you see the faulty rules and thus refuse to continue playing. No matter what you do, you cannot transcend your current level of consciousness, until you begin to question your perception filter—and your ego will do everything it can in order to prevent you from doing this.

The ego has created a false path, which we might call the outer path. It makes you think that you can qualify for the ascension by doing something to change other people or change the world. The real path is an inner path, where you realize that the *only* way that *you* can qualify for *your* ascension is to change yourself—your sense of self. And the only way to rise to a higher sense of self is to let the old self die. But in order to do that, you must come to see it as a limitation, see it as unreal and see that the Conscious You is more than the outer self, meaning that the Conscious You will not die when the self dies. And in order to come to that point, you must see through the smokescreen created by the ego.

THE LEVELS OF THE EGO

There are three major phases on the spiritual path. When you first descended to earth, you came in at the 48th level, meaning that you perceived the world through the perception filter that corresponds to that level of consciousness. At this level, you do have a sense that you are connected to something greater than yourself, but you do not have a clear perception of your I AM Presence. When you try to see the Presence, your vision is obscured by the veil formed by the seven rays.

You also have a sense that the world is a whole, meaning that what you do affects the whole and thus also yourself. You do not have a clear realization of why this is so, but you do have an intuitive sense of this, and thus there are certain choices that you simply will not make. At this level, you will not take actions that clearly harm others, because you sense this is not in your own best interest.

The Conscious You has free will, and it is charged with making choices based on its current perception filter. Thus, at the 48th level, you face a temptation to either rise higher or go lower, in order to create an upward spiral or a downward spiral. Below the 48th level of consciousness, you find levels that all have one characteristic: they are based on the

| 11 | *Escaping the prison of the ego*

very subtle belief that you are a separate being, meaning you can harm others without affecting yourself.

The effect is that when you enter those levels, you lose the sense that you are connected to your spiritual self and that you are connected to all life. In other words, once you go below the 48th level, the ego that you create will make it seem believable, that you are a separate being, living in a world of separate things and people. You are also separated from God, which means the ego makes it seem like you can do something and either get away with it or hide it from God. This allows you to do things you wouldn't do if you saw yourself as an extension of God. It now seems justifiable for you to do the things that only a separate being can do—namely act as if you have a right to do what you want, regardless of the consequences this has for others. You then start acting as if the ends can justify the means.

The ego has created a false path: the outer path. It makes you think that you can qualify for the ascension by doing something to change other people or change the world.

The inevitable companion to this state of consciousness is a sense of being alone and of being threatened by other people or material conditions. Thus, it is inevitable that you deal with the sense of being threatened by seeking to control your environment, including other people. As you look at the lower levels of consciousness, you see people who become increasingly controlling and willing to dominate others, even willing to kill those they cannot control.

For these people, such behavior seems perfectly justifiable and necessary, and the reason is that they are completely identified with the ego that corresponds to their level of consciousness. Thus, they believe in the perception they have through the ego, meaning they see their behavior as perfectly justifiable, necessary or unavoidable. At the lowest levels

The Power of Self

of consciousness, you find people who are absolutely convinced that their behavior is justified by some higher cause. Obvious examples are Hitler, Stalin and Mao, who saw it as fully justifiable to kill any number of people in order to manifest their vision of a better world. We can now see that there are three distinct levels of ego:

- Below the 48th level we find an ego that is aggressively seeking to control and dominate other people. Such people are struggling against something outside themselves. This level of ego also aggressively seeks to make decisions for you—or at least to control the decisions made by the Conscious You. The ego is doing this because it has a specific outlook on life, and it might be called the "deficit approach." Because this ego sees itself as a separate being, it must by necessity feel incomplete. And thus it is always seeking to make up for this incompleteness by taking something from others or by getting other people – even God – to do it some kind of favor. This ego is always looking for a savior from outside itself, but of course, it never finds that savior. It is seeking to force the entire universe to conform to its mental box, but the universe stubbornly refuses to play along.

- Between the 48th and the 96th level, we find an ego that is not aggressive and controlling towards others, as much as it is seeking to control you. Most spiritual people are at this level, which means they are struggling against something inside themselves.

- Between the 96th and the 144th level we find an ego that is more subtle. This is where you strive to find the delicate balance of not allowing the material realm to have power over you – as you come to see yourself as Spirit – while at the same time building complete respect for the free will of other people—not falling for the temptation of forcing them to grow but only seeking to inspire them through example.

The bottom line is that the ego can be seen as a filter that colors your perception. When you are at the lowest level of consciousness, there are

| 11 | *Escaping the prison of the ego*

144 layers of this perception filter. This has two implications. First of all, it is impossible to have a direct experience of the pure light that descends from your I AM Presence. The Conscious You is so identified with its level of consciousness, that it is very difficult for it to experience itself as pure awareness, and thus it cannot "see" that it is more than its sense of self. (That is why some people are ready to kill others in order to preserve their unreal sense of self.) Secondly, the Conscious You is completely convinced that its perception is real, and even that it has a right to define what is real and unreal.

In this state of mind, you are generally unreachable for a spiritual teacher, especially the ascended masters. Yet this does not mean you are "lost" and have no way back. However, it does mean that you can learn in only one way: through what the masters call the "School of Hard Knocks." You learn by constantly struggling against some opposition, until you finally come to the point of thinking: "I have had enough of struggling against this, there must be a better way, there must be more to life."

This can cause you to shift your consciousness to a higher level, where you struggle against something else, until you have had enough of that experience. And eventually, you can then climb to the 48th level, where you will be open to receiving instructions from the ascended masters through your intuition. This is when you begin to realize, that instead of seeking to change God, the world or other people, you need to change your sense of self.

As you continue to climb, you peel away layers of perception filters, and this continues to the 144th level, where you shed the final layer and can no longer maintain a physical body, so you ascend to the spiritual realm.

There is, however, an important shift that occurs at the 96th level, because at this level you begin to have direct perception of your vertical oneness with your I AM Presence. This is what we might call the Alpha aspect of Christhood. At this point, you have attained some mastery of mind over matter, because you know how to use the seven rays out of which all matter is made.

The Power of Self

The question now becomes how you use that mastery, especially how respectful you are of other people. The temptation you face is to use your powers frivolously to prove something to others or even using them to force others. This was illustrated by Jesus in the situation where he was tempted by the devil after fasting for 40 days in the wilderness.

Jesus came to give humankind an example of a person who is above the 96th level, where "I and my father are one."

At the 96th level you begin working on the Omega aspect of Christhood, namely your horizontal oneness with all life. This means that while you now become completely willing to serve others, you never seek to force them, even if you see that it would be "for their own good" to do so. Instead, you completely respect the principle of free will, and you allow others to grow by making their own choices.

Jesus actually came to give humankind an example of a person who is above the 96th level. That is why he said: "I and my father are one" (vertical oneness) and "inasmuch as ye have done it to the least of these my brethren, ye have done it unto me" (horizontal oneness).

At the 96th level, you have an intuitive sense that all life is one, and as you grow to higher levels, you being to directly see the reality that all life is one. This is when you can begin to see through the perception filter created by the mind of anti-christ, namely that all life is separate. This lie of separation is the ultimate lie that you must overcome before you can ascend—as this lie is not found in the ascended realm. The illusion of separation is possible in the material realm only because the density of matter makes it seem plausible that "things" are separate and that the material world is separated from God.

Let us briefly tie this in to what was said about the soul. When the Conscious You first descended at the 48th level, there was an ego that was

| 11 | *Escaping the prison of the ego*

part of the self you took on at that level. If (and not all have done this) you made the choice to go below the 48th level, you created another layer of ego, namely the more aggressive one that seeks to control others. This ego now becomes part of your soul, and you will carry it with you from lifetime to lifetime until you transcend it.

THE SUBCONSCIOUS MIND

The subconscious mind is a highly complex topic, so there is no simple way for you to understand or deal with your subconscious mind. There are many teachings (in psychology, self-help and spirituality) that will tell you that they have a simple and easy program for helping you overcome all of your problems. However, once you begin to understand the subconscious mind, you will see why there is no quick-fix. You will also, however, see that there is a viable long-term path to transcendence.

The teachings of the ascended masters can help you by giving you the awareness that there are four levels of the subconscious mind, corresponding to the identity level, the mental level, the emotional level and the physical level. Furthermore, these levels form a hierarchical structure, meaning that nothing in the physical mind can override what is in the emotional mind and so on. Why is this important? Well, if you are to master your life, you need to take command over your subconscious mind. The reason being that for many people, it is the subconscious mind that determines how they react to most situations. And the subconscious mind is nothing more than a sophisticated computer.

CREATING A COMPUTER PROGRAM

Consider a common life experience. If you repeat a certain action enough times, you create a "computer program" in the subconscious mind, that can now perform the action without your conscious mind being engaged in it. One example is riding a bicycle; once you have learned it, you never forget it. You might not ride a bike for ten years, but once you get on a bike, the subconscious computer program takes over.

The important point here is that if you are exposed to a certain situation enough times, and if you react the same way each time, then the subconscious computer will create a program based on the assumption, that you always want to react the same way to similar situations. And once such a program has been created, it will lie dormant in the subconscious mind, waiting for a situation that triggers it into action. Once that happens, the program will now take over your reaction to the situation, and it will do everything in its power to neutralize your conscious will power. Which is why so many people feel they have no conscious ability to override these reactionary patterns.

Once a subconscious program has been created, it will lie dormant in the subconscious mind, waiting for a situation that triggers it into action.

The real problem here is that many of these programs were created in the past, either in past lives or in childhood. As an example, consider a common program. As a child, you were exposed to an authority figure, such as a parent or teacher, who was verbally abusive towards you. You built a subconscious program based on you submitting to the abuse without defending yourself. This was a reasonable reaction for a child, who had very limited options, because you could neither speak out nor walk away from the situation. Yet once the program is in the subconscious computer, it will stay there for lifetimes.

So when you – as an adult or lifetimes later – encounter an authority figure who is verbally abusive, the subconscious program is triggered, and you now respond the same way you did when the program was created. The problem here is that as an adult you have better options than as a child. You can indeed speak out or walk away, but the program is not based on these options, so it can only continue to repeat the same reaction indefinitely.

| 11 | *Escaping the prison of the ego*

Of course, the belief in your mind has the effect of acting like a filter, and this filter will color or qualify the energy that streams through your mind. As explained earlier, lower energies cannot rise back to the I AM Presence, which means they will begin to accumulate in your energy field, in your four lower "bodies." You now have a pattern where a dysfunctional belief has been reinforced over a long time by the very energies qualified through the belief. So in order to break free of the pattern, you have to overcome both the energies and the belief. This is quite easy to do, once you have the knowledge and the tools provided by the ascended masters. However, without this knowledge, breaking these old patterns is extremely difficult.

THE WAY OUT

The only way you can break out of the pattern is to use your conscious mind, and this is where most people get trapped in an approach, that is either not very effective or actually adds to their problems. This approach is that you seek to use your conscious will power to override the subconscious programming. This is indeed possible, but it comes at a cost.

Let us look at a concrete example. A man has a subconscious program that makes him believe he is inferior, and whenever a situation triggers this belief, he feels unbearable emotional pain. Because he believes there is no way to avoid the pain, the only option he can see is to dull his mind, so he doesn't feel the pain as much. So he takes a drink, which eventually leads to other situations that trigger his sense of inferiority.

The man finally has a shocking experience that makes him realize he cannot continue to drink, and he makes a firm decision to stop drinking. So he uses his conscious will power to be alert for the impulse to drink, and then he overrides it before acting upon it. In the beginning, this requires a herculean effort, but after a while it becomes easier. The reason is that the man has now created a new subconscious program designed to override the previous program.

The obvious drawback is that the original program is still in the subconscious mind. The new program can override it in situations that the man has so far encountered, but at any time he could encounter a new situation, where the old program is able to override the new one, so he lapses back into drinking.

Is there an alternative approach? Obviously, and it is to realize that the subconscious program starts with a specific limiting belief. You can now use the Conscious You's ability to peal back the veil of the subconscious mind and examine the original program. Once this program is seen for what it is, it will be seen to originate from a decision. And once you see that the decision is dysfunctional, you can use the Conscious You's ability to replace it with a better decision, whereby the original program is dissolved.

We might say that the Conscious You did make the original decision, but then the decision descended below the level of conscious awareness. Yet at any time, the Conscious You has the ability to expand the sphere of what it is consciously aware of. The Conscious You can do this because it has not been changed by any decision it made. Thus, it can never lose the ability to project itself outside its current sense of self.

This truly is a viable approach. In fact, it is the *only* viable approach to permanent progress towards self-mastery—which is the foundation for mastering your circumstances in the material world. The only drawback is that this is not a quick-fix. It takes time and it takes effort—but first of all it takes a willingness to look into the subconscious mind and to make better decisions.

TRANSCENDING SUBCONSCIOUS PROGRAMS

Let us again look at the man who responds to an inferiority complex by drinking. The drinking is a physical action, and it may be triggered by a subconscious program in the body mind, a program that triggers his physical body into craving the effects of alcohol. And although this craving can be difficult to deal with and may require physical measures, it was originally triggered by a program in the higher levels of the mind. Each

| 11 | *Escaping the prison of the ego*

level of the mind program starts with a belief, which is why the higher way to overcome the program is to make the belief conscious—and then change it consciously.

At the physical level, there might be various beliefs that all seem to justify or necessitate taking a drink in order to get some relief. Yet at the bottom of them will be a sense that you are powerless to escape the emotional pain, so the only way out is to not experience anything. Once you realize this, you can see that this program is based on the belief that you cannot avoid the emotional pain. In a sense, this is correct, because at the level of the physical mind you cannot resolve or stop the emotional pain.

However, the Conscious You is *not* the physical mind; it is more than the physical mind. Thus, once you make use of the Conscious You's ability to project itself beyond its current level, you will indeed be able to see how to deal with the emotional level. We might say that as long as the Conscious You looks at your situation through the filter of the body mind, it will seem impossible to avoid the emotional pain. Yet once the Conscious You expands its self-awareness to a higher level, it will be perfectly capable of changing emotional reactions.

Let me say this another way. If the Conscious You is identified with the physical body, it is looking at the emotional mind from below, and from this position it simply cannot change the emotional mind. Yet if the Conscious You makes use of its ability to project itself up into the emotional mind, it is now looking at this mind from the same level. And from this level, the Conscious You does have the power to change an emotional pattern.

Once you recognize this, you can reason that if the pain starts at the emotional level, you can push back the veil and take a conscious look into the emotional body. If you can resolve it there, then there will no longer be emotional pain and thus no reason to dull your mind.

There is, of course, one drawback to this approach, and it is that when you start consciously looking into the emotional mind, you will encounter the emotional pain stored there, and it can be both scary and overwhelming. In fact, many people will go into the emotional mind only because something (such as drinking) has caused so much emotional pain, that they are willing to endure the extra pain in the short term in order to change their lives in the long term.

However, the ascended masters offer you another option. A subconscious program starts with a belief that acts like throwing a boulder into a stream. Mud, rocks and debris will start accumulating behind the boulder, so that from downstream you cannot even see the boulder. However, the "debris" in the mind is simply energy. This energy originally came from your I AM Presence, but it was given a lower vibration (misqualified) by the limiting belief.

The Conscious You is not the physical mind.
Once you make use of the Conscious You's ability to
project itself beyond its current level, you will indeed be
able to see how to deal with the emotional level.

When you start looking into the emotional mind, you will first encounter a reservoir of emotional energy, and it will either overwhelm you or prevent you from seeing the dysfunctional belief hiding behind the energy. As explained, the masters have given us tools to raise the vibration of this energy (transmute or re-qualify it), namely to invoke spiritual energy through decrees and invocations. By doing this, you can go into the emotional mind while feeling little or no pain, and you can more easily uncover the underlying belief.

Once you uncover a limiting belief in the emotional mind, you will see that it is actually based on an impulse coming from the mental mind. For example, the emotional mind might believe that in certain situations, you clearly are inferior, and thus there is no other reaction than to feel bad about yourself.

Yet you can now begin to examine this belief, and you will find that it involves a certain sense of having no other option, of feeling stuck. You can then begin to examine where this belief comes from, and this will take you into the mental mind. Again, you will encounter some

| 11 | *Escaping the prison of the ego*

misqualified energy, but instead of feeling emotional pain, it will cause you to feel doubt and confusion. And again, this energy can be dissolved by using specific tools for transforming energy.

Eventually, you can uncover the deeper beliefs in the mental mind, and they will often relate to a world view in which there are two kinds of people: those who are superior (authority figures) and those who are inferior and thus can never actually rise above their current position.

You can then begin to ask yourself where this belief comes from, and this can take you to the identity level, the highest level of the mind. This is where you will likely uncover a belief that says you are a fundamentally limited and powerless being. You might find the belief that you are a human being, with all the limitations that implies. You might also find a belief that you belong to a lower class of beings who are subservient to other beings or that you are a sinner by nature, that you are somehow fundamentally flawed.

Again, you will encounter certain very dense and heavy energies, but they can also be transmuted. And once you begin to question the beliefs you encounter, you can become aware that you are the Conscious You, and you are an extension of your I AM Presence. As such, it gives no meaning to evaluate yourself based on a relative, dualistic scale with inferior and superior. You are a unique being, and in uniqueness there are no comparisons. You can also become aware that you are a spiritual being, who cannot be affected by human limitations. Thus, you were not created as a sinner or with a fundamental flaw.

Obviously, there are many dysfunctional beliefs at the four levels of the mind, and they have been built up over many lifetimes. You will also have to deal with the collective consciousness, which has also been built up over a long period of time. Nevertheless, by being persistent and by using all means available (such as therapy and self-help techniques plus the tools given by the ascended masters) you can indeed make real progress. And considering that the subconscious beliefs have been built over many lifetimes, it truly is amazing that you have the potential to overcome all of them in one lifetime—if you apply yourself to the process.

The Power of Self

HOW THE EGO COMPLICATES THE PROCESS

It is helpful to be aware that the ego will complicate this process, if you are not aware of how the ego works. The basic problem is that the ego can have power over you only as long as it can stay hidden from your conscious awareness. And where is the best way for the ego to hide from you? In the subconscious mind, of course. Which means that the ego will prefer that your subconscious mind stays SUB-conscious.

The ego will make many decisions for you, but there are some decisions that only you can make. It is important to keep this in mind, because the only way to neutralize the ego is to realize that in the past, you decided that there were certain decisions that you did not want to make—and thus you allowed the ego to make those decisions for you.

The only way to break the grip of the ego is to consciously decide that you are willing to make these decisions. Yet the original decision to not make decisions was caused by the fact, that in certain situations it seemed like there was no good decision, and thus no way to avoid negative emotions. With proper tools you can neutralize the emotional energy, and by seeking greater attunement with your higher self, you can become able to see more options, so you realize there is always a decision that leads to growth.

If we reach back to the example of the man who was drinking, we can realize something important about all forms of escapism. The basic lie of the ego is that looking into your subconscious mind is either dangerous or unnecessary. For example, many people feel deeply affected by emotional pain, but they believe the ego's lie that looking into their emotions will only cause more pain. This puts them in a catch-22, because they now see no option for resolving the emotional pain. It seems as if their only option is to not feel anything, and thus they must dull their minds.

So the subtle lie of the ego is that the only way to avoid the pain is to not be conscious. The only way to not feel the pain is to not feel anything. Yet in reality, the only way to permanently transcend the pain is to become *more* conscious. The core of your being is called the *Conscious*

| 11 | *Escaping the prison of the ego*

You because its most basic characteristic is that it is conscious, it is aware. It is only by becoming more aware of the subconscious mind that you can resolve the beliefs that cause you pain. Which is why the path offered by the ascended masters is a path of gradually becoming more and more conscious, until all that is hidden has been revealed. For when you fully see a subconscious belief, you will also see that you are more than that belief, and this will make it easy for you to transcend the belief. It really is very simple: All limitations are lies. When you see that a belief is a lie, you also see the truth that sets you free from the lie. You simply cannot know that an idea is a lie without seeing the truth. And the truth will set you free.

THE BODY MIND

In order to complete the picture of the subconscious mind, we need to look at an element which the ascended masters call the body mind. This name indicates that it is a level of the mind that is related to the functions of the physical body. For example, you do not have to consciously tell your heart to beat or your cells to produce protein. Imagine having to be consciously aware of the function of each of the trillions of cells in your body, having to tell them what to do. You would never have any conscious attention left over for actually doing anything with your physical body, let alone enjoying life.

So, in a sense the body mind is simply like a supercomputer that controls the functions of the enormously complex physical body, that the Self uses as a vehicle for expressing itself in the material world. The problem is that the supercomputer can actually take on a life of its own, as you might have read in some science-fiction books.

The bottom line is this: The body mind is a computer that is designed to help you use your physical body. Yet if you do not pay attention – and of course, none of us were brought up with this knowledge – the servant might actually become your master. And that definitely will not facilitate your spiritual growth.

The Power of Self

In many religious and even some spiritual teachings, the physical body is portrayed as being evil or at least the enemy of your spiritual growth. This is not what the ascended masters teach. They teach that the physical body is a vehicle for our spiritual growth, and as such we should honor it and take care of it. However, we also need to not allow the body and its desires to run our lives.

The body mind is a supercomputer that controls the functions of the enormously complex physical body, that the Self uses as a vehicle in the material world.

We do this by being aware that the computer that runs the body is not actually able to think. Thus, it simply runs programs, and it will continue to run them until our conscious minds set limits. For example, the body has certain basic needs, and the body mind will seek to fulfill those needs without any humanitarian or spiritual considerations.

One basic need is protection, and to the body mind, there is nothing wrong with killing or in other ways neutralizing anything that seems like a danger, including other human beings. You will see some dictators or crime bosses that indiscriminately kill anyone who is perceived as a threat—without ever considering whether the perception is realistic. The reason is that such people have allowed the body mind to take over their lives—at least in this aspect.

Another example is food. The body mind will eat any food that is available or that it likes, and it will eat as much of it as it can. It cannot restrict itself, and that is why you see some people who overeat or eat unhealthy foods—their body minds are running their eating behavior.

Another basic need is propagation. The body mind has no limit to how much sex you can have, and (at least for men) it is actually programmed to seek as much sex as possible and with as many different partners as possible. Thus, you see some people who think they are sophisticated because they go beyond the traditional pattern of having only

| 11 | *Escaping the prison of the ego*

one sexual partner, but they simply don't realize that their lives are being run by the body mind.

How do you avoid having your life run by the body mind? It will happen as part of the process of going into the subconscious mind. The body mind is meant to be your servant, meaning you define the boundaries for how you will allow the body mind to deal with food, sex or security. Some people did – at some point in the past – decide that they did not want to make conscious decisions about this, so they let the body mind take over. Yet behind this was a belief, and once you uncover the belief, you can take control away from the body mind and again set your conscious boundaries.

As always, the key is to increase your awareness and purify your four lower bodies from misqualified energy. What we normally call a craving is a magnetic pull on our emotional body that comes from the physical body. It is caused by an accumulation of misqualified energy, and as you invoke spiritual light to transform that energy, the craving will naturally diminish. And as you become more aware of how the subconscious mind works, you will build the ability to resist the cravings of the body mind and turn this computer into the servant of your spiritual growth that it was designed to be.

CHAPTER 12

OTHER ASPECTS OF THE SELF

We earlier talked about the need to transform your inner experience, your Life Experience. In this chapter we will look at how you can use the knowledge about the components of self to accomplish this transformation. Let us begin by looking at an aspect of your I AM Presence that we briefly mentioned earlier.

YOUR CAUSAL BODY

One of the amazing effects of studying the teachings of the ascended masters is that you realize nothing is ever wasted. It is so easy to look at our lives and feel like we have gone through so much nonsense and so many unpleasant situations that we have wasted time and energy. Yet when you understand how your I AM Presence deals with your experiences, you see that anything can be turned into a positive learning experience.

On Image 12 (see the next page), you will see a number of rings (in reality, they are spheres) around the sphere that represents your I AM Presence. These rings represent the attainment you have gathered through your journey in the material world, the mastery you have attained on the seven spiritual rays. In a colored image, each ring has the color of the corresponding ray.

| 12 | Other aspects of the Self

Image 12- Your Causal Body forms rings around your I AM Presence

This mastery is a product of your positive learning experiences—and take note that even what seems like a mistake can be turned into a positive learning experience. Whatever you do here below, your Presence can learn from it and incorporate the lesson in your causal body.

In other words, when you identify yourself as a limited self, you are immersed in that self and the limitations it defines. Yet even though this is a limited experience, once you awaken to the realization that you are not the lower self, your experience becomes positive. You realize that you are more than the limited self, and once you have had that experience enough times, you will begin to realize that you are more than any self in this world.

Thus, it is wise to look at life as a scientific experiment and understand the ideal relationship between your I AM Presence and the Conscious You. The Conscious You does indeed have free will, and it makes choices based on its perception in the material world. Thus, as long as it identifies itself with the outer self, the Conscious You can only make decisions based on the perception filter that defines this self—and through which it sees everything.

This means not only that the Conscious You makes decisions based on its perception, but also that it evaluates the outcome of those decisions based on its perception filter. Thus, you judge yourself based on the same perception filter that caused you to make a certain decision. This is what Jesus called "judging after appearances."

The Power of Self

In contrast, your Presence does *not* see the world through your perception filter. It sees through the crystal clarity of the mind of Christ, and it does *not* judge you as you judge yourself (or as other people judge you). This is why Jesus told us that unless we become as little children, we cannot enter the kingdom of God. The kingdom of God is a metaphor for a state of consciousness, in which the Conscious You sees itself as an extension of the Presence.

This means you are no longer judging yourself through the perception filter of the outer self; you are seeing your choices and their consequences as your Presence sees them. And this is the *only* way to transcend the crippling guilt we have all been exposed to and which tends to paralyze us.

The causal body becomes a storehouse for all of our positive learning experiences. Once you begin to tune in to it through your intuition, you can draw upon the experiences you have had in past lifetimes. And this is why so many spiritual people have an inner knowing of what is right, even though they cannot always explain with the outer mind why they know it is right.

Your causal body can be seen as your cosmic database, that can empower you to make the best possible decisions in any situation you encounter on earth. You can draw upon your experiences of all similar situations you have encountered in past lives. Take note that this may not necessarily happen with full conscious knowledge of past lives, but through an inner knowing of what is the right thing to do.

It is obvious that this is a better foundation for making decisions than the knowledge you have from your current perspective. You also have in your causal body a storehouse of correctly qualified energy, and when you learn to unlock it, the energy will give you a positive momentum for manifesting the kind of life circumstances you want here on earth. We might say that the combination of wisdom and momentum from your causal body is the true power of Self.

So how do you unlock this creative potential? Well, you must remove the filters that block your oneness with the Presence. As we have discussed, the soul also acts as a storehouse for both experiences and

| 12 | *Other aspects of the Self*

energy. Yet the experiences stored in the soul are the ones based on your limited perception. And the energies stored in the soul are the ones qualified based on limited beliefs and frustrated emotions.

Unlocking your creative potential means that you remove the filters that block your oneness with the Presence.

Your soul also has a database, and most people draw on their negative experiences from past lives in order to make decisions. They often act based on the momentum of misqualified emotions stored in their emotional bodies, which explains why people are often running away from something they fear without knowing why they fear it. The result is, as the headlines of any day will prove, that people keep acting out the same negative patterns that have been dominating this planet for most of its history.

As we have seen, the ascended masters offer a viable, systematic path for transcending these age-old patterns. As you begin to expand your awareness and purify your four lower bodies, you will gradually become able to overcome the past momentums. Yet this becomes much easier when you understand the need to consciously examine your past momentums and to consciously choose that you want to make decisions based on the database of your causal body rather than the database of the soul.

YOUR CHRIST SELF

On the following image, the figure that sits at the nexus of the figure-eight is your Christ self. It is the mediator between the I AM Presence and the lower being lost in duality, specifically the Conscious You.

The Power of Self

Image 13 - Your Christ Self in the nexus of the figure eight flow as the mediator between the I AM Presence and the lower being.

We might say that your Christ self is a spiritual teacher that is sent to those who descend below the 48th level of consciousness. These people are now so focused on the material realm, that they lose the direct, inner sense of being connected to their I AM Presences. Thus, they cannot receive instructions from the Presence or from the ascended masters.

The Christ self is created by ascended masters, who lay down part of their own energy in order to create a self that can descend and reach you in whatever state of consciousness you are at. This is done in order to fulfill an aspect of the cosmic Law of Free Will. This law says that you have the right to descend into any state of consciousness you want, but that you must always have a way to transcend that state of consciousness. Which means you must always have access to a frame of reference from outside the perception filter of your current sense of self. Thus, your Christ self will descend with you, and at any time you are willing to listen, it will offer you a way to rise above your current level of consciousness.

This is symbolized by the Christ taking physical embodiment as Jesus. The Christ self is inside your container of self, and thus you can hear it at any time by focusing on your heart and activating your intuitive faculties. Jesus talked about the Christ self in the following quotes:

| 12 | Other aspects of the Self

And I will pray the Father, and he shall give you another Comforter, that he may abide with you for ever; (John 14:16)

But the Comforter, which is the Holy Ghost, whom the Father will send in my name, he shall teach you all things, and bring all things to your remembrance, whatsoever I have said unto you. (John 14:26)

It does not take any superhuman or psychic abilities to hear the still, small voice of your Christ self. However, take note that your Christ self does *not* look at you or your life through your current perception filter. In fact, the purpose of your Christ self is to – in any situation – offer you an alternative to your current perception filter.

This does not mean that your Christ self offers you some absolute or ultimate truth, because your Christ self knows exactly what you can and cannot accept based on your current perception filter. Thus, the goal of your Christ self is to offer you a frame of reference that is one step above your current perception.

A GRADUAL PATH

Your Christ self knows that you need to follow a gradual, step-by-step path from your current level of consciousness to the full Christ consciousness. It is not seeking to get you to make this journey in one giant leap – as many spiritual seekers want and as some gurus claim they can do – it is seeking to help you take the next step, and then the next, and so on.

This means that there is *never* a situation, where your Christ self cannot reach you. You always have the option to hear your Christ self; the question is whether you are willing to open your mind and heart to something that is beyond your current perception filter. If you are not willing to reach beyond your perception filter, you will not be able to hear the voice of your Christ self. Instead, you will hear the louder voice of your ego, the mass consciousness or false teachers, who will tell you what you want to hear. Whether you seek confirmation of your current per-

The Power of Self

ception, or whether you seek a frame of reference beyond your current perception, you will always find what you seek.

There is never a situation, where your Christ self cannot reach you. You can always hear your Christ self; the question is whether you are willing to open your mind and heart to something that is beyond your current perception filter.

It is wise to be aware that our outer selves always want confirmation for what we are currently doing or what we currently believe. Since our Christ selves only seek to help us transcend our current state, they will never give us this validation. Which means that the more focused we are on getting validation, the less we will be able to hear the "still small voice" of our Christ selves.

Your Christ self is not trying to make you comfortable; it is seeking to help you grow. Your ego is seeking to stop your growth, and thus it will tell you what makes you feel comfortable, if that can keep you under the ego's control. (The ego might also manipulate you into being very uncomfortable, if that will help it control you.)

Be aware that your ego is always seeking to replace your Christ self. One way it does so is to get you to rationalize away your intuitive insights. In fact, your ego is constantly trying to set itself up as the ultimate authority in your life, a position that should be occupied by your Christ self until the Conscious You attains a direct connection to your Presence. The ego does this by setting up certain beliefs as being beyond questioning, thereby creating a mental box around your mind. Thus, many people dare not look beyond their mental boxes to hear the voice of their Christ selves. The Christ self is *always* seeking to lead you outside *any* mental box and thus it challenges the "infallible" beliefs of the ego.

As you follow the spiritual path, you gradually put on the mind of Christ, meaning that you gain the vision and discernment that empowers

| 12 | *Other aspects of the Self*

you to see through the many illusions created by the mind of anti-christ. This helps you reclaim the purity of your Self from the selfish beliefs that cause your suffering. It is through the mind of Christ that you can take dominion, first over your Self, and then over the material realm.

At first, the Conscious You will see your Christ self as an external teacher, but you will gradually build a deeper sense of oneness with the teacher. This leads to the mystical union, whereby you become the bride of Christ and attain oneness with your I AM Presence. You can then accept that the Conscious You has attained its rightful position as the Christ in your being. You have become the Living Christ.

You will then be "As Above, so below," meaning that your I AM Presence can now act through the I Will Be Presence that you have become. Your sense of identity in this world reflects your spiritual individuality, anchored in your Presence.

You have then taken dominion over the earth, as symbolized by the globe under the feet of the Vitruvian man in Image 14.

You can then claim with Jesus, "My Father worketh hitherto, and I work" (John 5:17).

Image 14 - The Vitruvian man and dominion over the earth

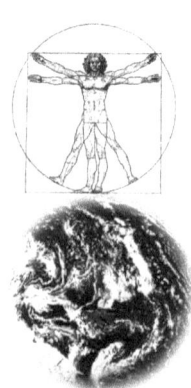

In your current state, the Conscious You has descended into the lower self and is identifying itself as the outer self. It is this identification that causes you to see a separation or distance between yourself and the I AM Presence. As you attain Christhood, the Conscious You ascends to the nexus of the figure-eight and occupies the position now held by your Christ self. Yet this dissolves the distance, and thus you have transcended the old state. You are now "as Above, so below," as depicted in Image 15.

The Power of Self

Image 15 - By attaining Christhood, the Conscious You ascends to the nexus of the figure-eight and occupies the position now held by your Christ self.

PART FOUR

A CLOSER LOOK AT THE SPIRITUAL PATH

CHAPTER 13

CHOOSING TO SHIFT YOUR LIFE EXPERIENCE

Perhaps the description of your total being has made you realize, that the spiritual path is more complex than you thought and requires more work than you had imagined? If so, do not feel overwhelmed. As we have discussed, there is a systematic way to improve your life. However, it is also possible to change your view of life, which can have an immediate effect on your well-being.

There are many spiritual or religious teachings that promise you an easy way out, an automatic path to salvation. In reality, the only true way is to systematically rebuild your sense of identity, until you accept who you truly are. This restores oneness between your higher being and the Self. This requires work; conscious work. You must purify your four lower bodies of all dualistic beliefs and misqualified energies. However, there is an easy way out—sort of.

The way out is to realize that the Conscious You, the Self, is what it thinks it is. Your Self has the ability to identify itself as anything it chooses, and it can change that sense of identity instantly. We might say that your ego has built a mental prison out of the self-centered beliefs and misqualified energies in your four lower bodies. You might think of this prison as a small brick box with just a tiny window in the door. The ego has then managed to trick the Self into entering that prison and believing it cannot escape. Thus, your Self is right now looking at the world and itself from the very limited perspective it has from inside the ego's

13 | Choosing to shift your experience

prison. This is what causes you to feel stuck, to feel that life is suffering and to feel like you have no way out.

In reality, the door to the prison is not locked. The Self can – at any time – decide to open it and step outside the prison. Doing this does not mean that the prison disappears. You must still undo the self-centered beliefs and the misqualified energies in order to take back control over your four lower bodies. Yet once you are outside the prison, your perspective on life will change dramatically.

You will no longer feel limited or stuck, and life will no longer seem like an endless process of suffering. You will realize the truth in the old saying, that you are not a human being trying to have a spiritual experience but a spiritual being having a human experience. And if you don't like the human experience you are having, you can change it by following the spiritual path.

You can use your Christ self as a guide to reclaiming your true identity. You will begin to realize and accept that you are a spiritual being, and you will begin to feel the freedom and joy that comes from knowing who you are, why you are here and how to fulfill your highest goals. The sole goal of the ascended masters is to give you the understanding and the tools that can help you claim this spiritual freedom.

WHY YOU ARE HERE RIGHT NOW

The state of oneness with your I AM Presence is your highest potential here on earth, and when you attain it, you can fulfill your rightful role as a co-creator with God. It is only when a critical mass of people attain this state of oneness, that the second coming of Christ can come about. This will bring God's kingdom into manifestation on earth, which will usher in a Golden Age of peace and enlightenment.

You most likely volunteered to come to earth at this particular time for the purpose of helping to bring in the Golden Age. You have most likely always had a sense that something isn't right on earth, that something is missing and that something needs to change. You most likely always had a longing for something better, something more, and that

The Power of Self

lost paradise is oneness with your I AM Presence. Thus, the key to your personal fulfillment and to improving the world, is to follow the ancient call: "Human, know thyself." Which really means: "Human, know thy Self as God." Your real self is your I AM Presence, and the Conscious You is the I Will Be aspect of the Presence.

In the past, you came to identify yourself as a limited self. How did you do this? You used the basic characteristic of the Conscious You, the Self. The Self is not created as a separate being. It is created in a polarity with the I AM Presence; it is created as the I Will Be aspect of the Presence. The I AM Presence says: "I AM" but the Self says "I Will be…" This means that the I AM Presence can be seen as the stable center, the sun, but the Self is a planet orbiting the sun. Thus, the Self is always moving, it is always transcending itself.

You will begin to realize and accept that you are a spiritual being, and you will begin to feel the freedom and joy that comes from knowing who you are, why you are here and how to fulfill your highest goals.

How did the self take on a lower sense of self at the 48th level or below? It said: "I will be that self," and then it suddenly was inside that self. So let us now say that you begin to awaken and you no longer want to be the limited self and suffer as that self suffers. How do you get out? Well, there are two dysfunctional approaches. One is that you need to see the self as an enemy and seek to destroy it. The other is that you need to perfect or raise the self, so that it will one day become acceptable to God.

The middle way beyond these two extreme approaches is to realize that the self is not real, and thus it has no power over the Self that is real. So what you need to do is to reconnect to the basic ability of the Conscious You, the ability to envision a higher self and then decide: "I will be that self." In other words, instead of seeking to do something with your

| 13 | *Choosing to shift your experience*

existing self (perfect or destroy it), you simply transcend it by projecting the Conscious You into a higher sense of self.

However, it is essential to realize that this is not a quick-fix. You will still have to transmute the energies that you generated through the former self. And you will still have to uncover and consciously replace the beliefs and decisions made through that self. Only then will you be able to permanently rise above the old self. Yet what you can do – and it can indeed happen instantly – is to use the Self's ability to be what you will be. This can indeed cause you to realize: "I am not the self that suffers, so who am I? I must be more than that self, and thus I am not stuck in the suffering." At that moment, you can break the spell of being identified with the lower self, which means that the suffering of that self will no longer seem as severe or as personal. You will know it is the lower self that suffers, not you, not the Conscious You.

The net effect of this is that you can instantly gain an entirely different perspective on yourself, your situation and on life. Instead of the deficit approach of feeling you are always behind or that you are flawed, you can begin to see life as a journey—and you can begin to enjoy the different aspects of the journey.

THE SHIFT CAN HAPPEN INSTANTLY

This shift in awareness can indeed happen instantly, however it is important to realize, that it may not happen just because you are reading this. If not, then the reason is that you still have so much misqualified energy in your four lower bodies, that the magnetic pull on your attention is too strong for you to break the spell of identification. And that is when you need to decide to follow the gradual path outlined by the ascended masters.

The masters are very practical. You might have noticed that there are some spiritual teachers on earth who claim that they had a spontaneous awakening experience. They experienced the sense of de-identification just described, and they did not think they had done anything to bring it about. In fact, some teachers will say there is nothing you can do.

The ascended masters say that there is no mechanical ritual that will force the awakening experience. Yet they also say that the natural state of the Conscious You, the Self, is to be in pure awareness. Thus, the only reason why you are not in pure awareness is that the magnetic pull of the outer self pulls your conscious awareness into identification with that self. So when you lessen that magnetic pull, there will eventually and inevitably come a point, when the Self will effortlessly – and seemingly without any conscious or mechanical effort – swing back to its natural state.

No mechanical ritual will force the awakening experience.

The masters say that when a person claims to have had a spontaneous awakening, the reason is that the person simply was not consciously aware of having gone through a process. The reason might be that the person took many steps in past lives, or that the person actually did question many beliefs without following a systematic teaching or procedure.

As the teachers who have fully awakened from the human level of consciousness, the ascended masters say that awakening is always a process. And by becoming consciously aware of how the process works, you can indeed do much to bring forward the moment, when you will "spontaneously" awaken from your identification with your present sense of self. You can bring forward the moment, where the Conscious You becomes conscious, where the Self realizes that it never lost the ability to be what it will be. Thus, it can always be more than it is right now.

IMMERSION AND AWAKENING EXPERIENCES

When you begin to realize who you really are – namely a Self that is an extension of your I AM Presence – you see that your higher self

13 | *Choosing to shift your experience*

made a choice to send the Self into embodiment on earth. This was not something you were forced to do; you did so for a positive purpose. The purpose was twofold:

- You wanted to express your spiritual individuality in this world. This was done partly for the pure joy of expressing yourself and also for the purpose of raising the material sphere. As explained earlier, self-aware beings grow by helping to raise their sphere so it can ascend and become part of the spiritual realm. And we help raise our sphere by letting the light and the qualities of our I AM Presences shine through our lower beings.

- You also wanted to experience this world as a way to help you grow. And we grow by taking on a limited self and then gradually growing beyond that self, realizing we are spiritual beings who cannot be defined by anything in this world. We grow by first thinking we are limited beings and then realizing we are more than such beings.

Think back to your experiences as a young child. You might have been afraid of the neighborhood bully, because you thought he would beat you up, and you felt too small to defend yourself. You might have been afraid of the neighbor's dog, because you thought it would bite you. Why did you have these childhood fears and concerns, and why did they seem so real to you? If you were to go back to those situations with your adult sense of self, what scared you back then would be no big deal today. So we now see that your childhood concerns seemed so real precisely because you identified yourself as a child, with all of the limitations that implied in your particular situation.

Now transfer this to life in general. You are an extension of a spiritual being, who cannot be limited by any condition on earth. Yet if you descended into embodiment with that awareness, where would be the learning experience? Thus, when you descend into physical embodiment, you go through a process of "forgetting" who you are. Instead, you take on an identity built based on the vibrations and the outer conditions found on earth. How does this happen?

The Power of Self

It happens because the Self or the Conscious You – which as we have seen is pure awareness – has the ability to project itself anywhere it wants. So the Conscious You projects itself into a particular sense of self (as a human being), and once it is inside that self, the self forms a perception filter, which is like putting on colored glasses. You see everything through the perception filter of your self, and thus you also see yourself through that filter. This means you "forget" that you are a spiritual being, and you believe – you perceive, and seeing is believing – that you really are a human being with all of the limitations defined by your self. This is what we might call an "immersion experience," because you are totally immersed in and identified with the material world.

The purpose of having an immersion experience is partially to provide a contrast to the spiritual realm, as that gives your I AM Presence a valuable perspective on the spiritual realm and how life functions. Yet the real purpose is to give you an opportunity to experience a growth in self-awareness. As we have said before, you start out with a point-like sense of self, and your potential is to expand it to the omni-present self-awareness of the Creator.

As the beginning of this process, you start out by having an immersion experience, where you truly believe that you are limited by the conditions in the material universe. Yet in an ideal scenario, you are meant to gradually expand your awareness of how the material world works and how you can use your creative abilities in this world. This means you will gradually realize that you are not a material being, but that you have the ability to create your own circumstances, rather than adapting to predefined conditions. This process is what we might call an "awakening experience," because it gives you a completely unique perspective on life. By starting out with a limited sense of self and then transcending that self, you tie in to the purpose of life itself. And you learn how to take conscious command over the process, so you can deliberately transform your sense of self.

This process of consciously transforming your sense of self is precisely what the Buddha, Jesus and all other true spiritual teachers came to demonstrate. The conclusion here is that life on earth can truly seem

| 13 | *Choosing to shift your experience*

very primitive, limiting and cruel. Yet if you look at it from a higher perspective, you see that no matter how primitive conditions might be, they still give us a unique opportunity to go through the basic process of personal growth, namely by first having an immersion experience and then having the experience of awakening from identification with that experience, coming to accept who we really are.

In an ideal scenario, you are meant to gradually expand your awareness of how the material world works and how you can use your creative abilities in this world.

You may look at your life and feel you have gone through many situations that you would rather have avoided. But what if this was all part of your immersion experience? And what if the greater purpose for those experiences was to demonstrate, that no matter how difficult conditions might be, you can still awaken from them and move to a higher level of self-awareness? What if you volunteered to take on these conditions precisely in order to demonstrate how to awaken from even the most intense immersion experiences? No matter how immersed you have been, you can always awaken.

Does this not give you a new perspective on life? Does it not give you a new sense of hope and purpose? Does it not give you a sense that with the teachings and tools offered by the ascended masters, you can truly leave behind any and all of the limiting experiences you have had on earth? And once you know you can leave something behind, it really doesn't seem quite as bad anymore, does it?

What the ascended masters offer is a systematic path, whereby you can awaken from *any* immersion experience and get on with doing what you came here for: demonstrate how to awaken to your spiritual potential and then how to express that potential.

CHAPTER 14

AN ASCENDED MASTER PERSPECTIVE ON KARMA

Most eastern religions teach the concept of karma, which is somewhat comparable to the Christian concept of sin. Many modern spiritual people are familiar with this concept, so what do the ascended masters say about karma? Isn't the spiritual path about balancing your karma?

The ascended masters certainly acknowledge the reality of karma, but they also teach that karma can be understood at different levels. Actually, this is a concept that it is very helpful to understand. The ascended masters teach that human beings are at many different levels of consciousness, and therefore one spiritual teaching simply cannot appeal to all. Consequently, the masters give different teachings for different levels of consciousness. So let us see how this applies to karma.

Some eastern religions portray karma as linked to your actions. If you take a certain action – such as killing another human being – you make bad karma. And if you take other types of action, you make good karma. In order to enter Nirvana, be saved or ascend, you have to balance all of the bad karma you have made in this and previous lifetimes. One way to balance bad karma is by having something bad happen to you, such as an accident, an illness or being killed. Another way is to compensate by making good karma, such as performing acts of service or charity. Most eastern teachings also say that there are other ways to balance karma. You can use various spiritual practices to neutralize the bad karma and thus more quickly qualify for entry into a higher realm.

| 14 | *An ascended master perspective on karma*

The ascended masters are not denying this teaching on karma and action. In the 1930's for example, a master called Saint Germain introduced the violet flame, which is a spiritual energy that is very suited for neutralizing karma. Saint Germain also gave a number of decrees for invoking the violet flame energy, as mentioned earlier.

However, take note that the teaching that karma is linked to action is based on not giving a very precise definition of what karma actually is. As we saw with the word "soul," many spiritual teachings use it without clearly defining it. And as with the concept of the soul, the ascended masters also give us a more sophisticated or layered understanding of karma.

In fact, the masters say that as humankind progresses, we go through various stages. During the time period of the Old Testament, we were indeed dealing with the initiations of reforming our outer actions, which corresponds to the teaching that karma is action. According to this level of teaching, you can be saved by avoiding actions that produce negative karma and performing actions that produce positive karma. This is what you see outpictured in the Old Testament in the form of the ten commandments, which basically said: "Thou shall not do this or that, and then thou shalt not make bad karma." You also had the concept of "an eye for an eye, and a tooth for a tooth," which is based on the idea that if you kill someone, then you deserve to be killed in order to neutralize the karma you made.

The ascended masters teach that this approach is indeed valid for a certain level of consciousness, as that is all people can grasp at that level. They do need to reform their outer actions in order to make less bad karma, and the only way to motivate them to do so is to give them the fear of what will happen to them, if they do not change their actions. So the teaching on karma as action is valid, but it is not the full story.

Humankind was actually meant to step up to a higher understanding of karma in the time period inaugurated by Jesus. You will note that Jesus went far beyond the Old Testament principle of "an eye for an eye," by telling us to turn the other cheek and forgive "seventy times seven." Jesus also told us that "the kingdom of God is within you," which has a very profound meaning. As mentioned before, the hidden meaning is that the "kingdom of God" is a metaphor for a certain state of consciousness. This means we will not enter the kingdom by simply performing outer actions; we also need to change our consciousness. In other words, Jesus came to teach us that balancing karma is not simply a matter of reforming outer actions; it also requires us to reform our state of mind.

With today's knowledge, we can take this one step further. Based on what we have discussed earlier, we can see that our actions always spring from conditions in our conscious and subconscious minds. In other words, we might take a certain action based on a decision we make with the conscious mind. However, that decision is not a neutral or free decision, because it is based on our perception. And what we perceive is not reality as it is; what we perceive is a mental image that is produced inside our minds. It is a product of the energies and beliefs that reside in the kaleidoscope of our minds. Based on this, we can now talk about three types of karma.

PHYSICAL KARMA

Because we now know that everything is energy, we can see, that we need to step up from the traditional view that karma is produced only by actions. If everything is energy, it means that everything we do is done with energy. In other words, even when we take a physical action, what we are really doing is to produce an energy impulse and direct it out from ourselves. We are sending the impulse into the universe.

Albert Einstein stated that the universe is made from something he called the "space-time continuum." He also said that this continuum can form closed loops. For example, Einstein theorized that if you travel away from the earth in a spaceship and keep going in the same direction, you will eventually return to your starting point from the opposite direction. The reason is that you are inside a loop in space-time, and you cannot escape it.

This image can help us understand how karma works. Planet earth is only the visible part of a larger energy field, or energy continuum. As we have already explained, there are four levels of this continuum, namely the etheric, mental, emotional and physical octaves. So let us say you perform a certain action, such as killing someone. That action produces an energy impulse that is sent into the energy loop inside which you live. It will then cycle through the four levels, and at some point it will come back to its point of origin (the physical world) from the opposite direction.

As the karmic energy impulse comes back, it can trigger certain events in your life, such as an accident, disease or being killed. If you do not believe in karma, it is difficult to explain such events. If you are a Christian, you might say it is God's punishment for your original sin, but that explanation is not satisfying for most spiritual people. If you are a materialist, you can only say this is the product of entirely random events. In either case, you are pacified, because what can you do to avoid such happenings? Once you accept karma, you become empowered, because now you can do something to avoid such events.

Once you understand that karma is an energy impulse, that you sent into the cosmic loop in a previous lifetime, you can see that you can do something to neutralize that energy impulse before it comes full circle and triggers an unpleasant even in your life. What can you do? You can learn how to use your God-given co-creative abilities to neutralize low-frequency energy.

Science has taught us that energy is a form of vibration that moves as a wave. As a visible example, take a tsunami. This is a wave that moves across the ocean. If you can create a wave that moves in the opposite direction, the two waves will meet and neutralize each other. When two waves meet, they form what scientists call an interference pattern. And if you match one wave to the vibrations of another wave, the interference pattern can be complete calm, meaning one wave neutralizes another wave.

This is the background for the concept of balancing karma through spiritual exercises. Such exercises produce a wave of high-frequency energy that you send into the four levels of the universe. As it travels out, it meets the wave of returning karma from a past lifetime. If you have sent out enough high-frequency energy, then the returning energy wave of your karma can be neutralized before it triggers a physical event. You can neutralize the returning karma in the etheric, mental or emotional realms before it descends into the physical realm.

Karma is an energy impulse, that you can neutralize before it comes full circle and triggers an unpleasant event in your life.

This is, of course, a wonderful teaching. Now all we have to do is perform a spiritual exercise – such as invoking the violet flame – and we will escape any bad karma from the past. And then we can live happily ever after, right? Well, not so fast.

MIND KARMA

The ascended masters teach that while karma certainly does have a physical component, namely an energy impulse sent into the universe, this is not all there is to karma. Karma also has a mental component, and we truly cannot escape our karma without dealing with the mental component. The reason is that you cannot escape the effect without changing the cause. And what produced the karmic impulse sent out in a past lifetime? It was the state of consciousness we had in that lifetime. Which means the real question is: "Have I transcended the state of consciousness that caused me to send out a certain karmic impulse?"

So what is karma? Well, in the West many spiritual people accept karma, but because of our Christian legacy of sin, we tend to see bad karma as a form of punishment. The ascended masters have a very different view of karma, as they know that no being in the spiritual realm has any desire to punish human beings. The masters know that God has no need to punish human beings, because God has given human beings free will.

14 | An ascended master perspective on karma

God has no opinion about how you should exercise your free will, because God simply wants you to learn, and God knows that the universe is set up so that you will inevitably learn from the way you exercise your free will. How does this happen? It happens because the Ma-ter light will take on the form of any mental images projected upon it. Thus, you will experience the consequences of any choice you make.

The purpose of the world is to provide us with a framework for expanding our self-awareness. We grow by exercising our co-creative abilities. We exercise our abilities by formulating a mental image, infusing it with the driving force of emotion and sending it into the universe (projecting it upon the Ma-ter light). Now, if doing this made no difference, how would we learn? So we learn because the Ma-ter light outpictures as physical forms and events the images we have projected upon it. In other words, karma is not punishment; karma is an opportunity to learn.

You formulate a mental image based on the contents of your identity and mental minds. You infuse it with energy in the emotional mind, and then you project it out, either as a purely psychic impulse or through a physical action. When the Ma-ter light gives you back physical circumstances that reflect what you sent out, you have an opportunity to evaluate. If what comes back is not pleasant, then you simply have to change what you are sending out. And then, the cosmic mirror will inevitably reflect back circumstances that outpicture the new image you are projecting into the mirror.

Do you see why neither God nor the ascended masters have any need to judge or punish you? You punish yourself by continuing to send out mental images that produce unpleasant physical circumstances. Yet the ascended masters do not condemn you for this. They simply stand eternally ready to help you produce better circumstances. The catch is that the masters simply cannot help you until you cross a very specific line, namely where you become open to at least considering that in order to change what comes back, you must change what goes out. The masters will not protect you from the consequences of your actions; they will help you change your actions and then the consequences will inevitably change.

The Power of Self

GETTING OUT OF A KARMIC HOLE

The problem is, of course, that if you have created bad karma over many lifetimes, you cannot expect that this can be changed in five minutes. And how can you even consider changing the contents of your mind, if you are constantly burdened by physical circumstances that are the result of your past karma? How can you worry about spiritual growth, when you are in a karmic hole and constantly fighting chaotic conditions?

The ascended masters know this, and that is precisely why the master Saint Germain asked for a cosmic dispensation, in order to be allowed to release knowledge of the violet flame. His reasoning was that as long as people are so burdened by their returning karma, they simply do not have attention left over for changing their state of consciousness, the state of consciousness that causes them to constantly make more karma.

Saint Germain saw that many people were in a karmic spiral, a spiritual catch-22, from which they could not escape. In past lifetimes, they had sent out karmic impulses that were returning to them in this lifetime. This karmic return caused certain events to take place in people's lives, and when this happened, people responded based on the very same state of consciousness they had when they sent out the karmic impulse. For example, say a person had killed someone in a past life. This karmic return came back in the form of a threat to the person's life. And the person then responded to this threat by fighting against other people, thereby continuing the karmic spiral.

Saint Germain's reasoning was that if people could get a relief from this intense karmic return, they might have enough attention left over for examining and changing their state of consciousness. Of course, there is no guarantee that they will use this reprieve to engage in self-examination, as they might also decide to enjoy their newfound freedom. And that is why Saint Germain had to get a dispensation from cosmic councils in order to release knowledge of the violet flame. Which brings us to the internal aspect of karma, where you can actually make karma with yourself.

| 14 | *An ascended master perspective on karma*

THE CAUSE OF KARMA

There is only one way for you to kill another human being. You must have become blinded by the illusion of separation, which makes you believe that you are a separate individual, and so is the other person. Thus, it seems believable to you that you can kill another human being without affecting yourself.

Yet in order for you to believe this, you must first have accepted a certain self-image. And once you have stepped into the perception filter of this separate self, you use it to constantly project the corresponding self-image upon yourself. Thus, you are constantly projecting that you are a separate being, and that means you also project that you are alone, have been abandoned by God, have limited powers—and that you are a victim of external conditions. There is always something "out there" that is controlling your life.

What we see now is that karma is actually made by people who perceive life through the perception filter of a separate self. Through this separate self you create a number of mental images, and you then turn them into energy impulses through the powers of your mind. Some of these impulses are sent out towards other people or the world. Yet some of them are sent inwards and projected upon yourself. This becomes your internal karma, the karma that stays inside your mind.

Once you understand this, it becomes clear that using a spiritual technique to neutralize returning karma is only a stage on your path towards spiritual freedom. In order to be truly free, it is not enough to free yourself from the karma that comes back to you. It is also necessary to free yourself from the perception filter through which you created the original impulses. If you do not transcend the separate self, you will simply continue to produce more karma, and thus you will not be able to break free of the cycle of rebirth.

It is like seeking to pay back a loan while spending more money than you make. If there is more money going out than you have coming in, how can you ever repay the loan? You will only truly balance karma when you stop making more karma. And you will accomplish this only when

The Power of Self

you free yourself from the illusion that you are a separate being, who is disconnected from your source.

NO AUTOMATIC WAY TO BALANCE KARMA

Take note of a subtle truth that few people understand. The real way to spiritual freedom is to transcend the illusion of separation. Accepting a spiritual teaching and practicing a spiritual technique will not make this happen automatically. It is a process that you must go through by expanding your awareness and making conscious decisions. So we can now outline three stages of the spiritual path:

- The lowest is the level where you seek to reform your physical actions through the fear of what will happen to you if you do certain things. This is the Old Testament level: "Thou shalt not" and "an eye for an eye."

- The next step is where you recognize the need to not only refrain from negative actions but also to become a better person. This is the level of the New Testament, often called the Age of Pisces. The problem is that this can lead to a blind alley, where you think that all you need to do is to become a good person according to a standard defined by an external religion or spiritual teaching. For example, you might think that bad karma can be neutralized by performing good karma.

- The next level, which is the level for the coming age of Aquarius, is where you recognize the need to fundamentally change your consciousness and escape the illusion of separation. You begin to realize that the real problem is the separate self. The illusion that you were a separate being was what caused you to make bad karma, such as killing people.

Many spiritual people have attempted to compensate for this by seeking to turn the separate self into a spiritual persona that never does bad things. Yet you are essentially seeking to use the separate self in order to compensate for the bad things done through the separate self. And this can never work. The separate self can never make it to the ascended realm.

In order to be truly free, it is not enough to free yourself from the karma that comes back to you. It is also necessary to free yourself from the perception filter through which you created the original impulses.

Thus, it is not a matter of making the separate self appear to be good according to some external teaching. It is a matter of transcending the separate self, letting it die, so the real Self returns to the pure awareness with which it descended. Only through this pure awareness can you avoid making karma—either good or bad.

When you begin to grasp these ideas, you can step up to a higher realization about karma. Karma is *any* impulse you project through the separate self. It does not matter whether the impulse is good or bad according to some earthly standard. In fact, the very concepts of good and bad are the products of the separate self and its dualistic form of thinking. There is a level on the spiritual path where it is necessary to believe, that the way to be saved is to avoid making bad karma and to make good karma. Yet the next level up is where you realize that even good karma will keep you from ascending, especially it if causes you to feel you are better than others.

Anything done through the separate self produces karma. Yet when you transcend the separate self, you can perform actions without making karma—good or bad. And that is spiritual freedom. We now see the higher view of karma. You have indeed produced karmic impulses in past lives, and they will eventually cycle back to you. It is perfectly valid to use spiritual techniques to consume these energy impulses before they return as physical events.

Yet you also need to work on freeing your mind from all of the illusions that spring from the consciousness of separation. These illusions form the colored glass pieces in the kaleidoscope of your mind, and as long as they remain, the light from your I AM Presence will be colored by them. Which means you are constantly sending out energy impulses colored by the contents of the four levels of your mind.

In other words, until all four levels of your mind are cleared from illusions, you are continually making karma. So the path offered by the ascended masters is a path of helping you rise above all karma from the past and all karma from the present. It is a path that can give you freedom from your own karmic spirals, so they do not continue to be self-reinforcing.

KARMA AND THE SEVEN RAYS

As we have seen, we make karma by sending out an energy impulse, but we do not produce that impulse. We cannot create energy, but what we can do is to qualify the energy we receive through our I AM Presences, the energy that comes from the ascended masters above us. And this energy comes in the form of the seven spiritual rays.

Each of the seven rays has a certain form of energy or vibration. Yet it also has certain other characteristics, such as power, wisdom or love. Making karma has two aspects. The first one is that you take the pure energy of one of the seven rays, and you lower its vibration below a critical level. Yet how do you lower the vibration of energy? You do so by forming a mental image, and it is like a film strip in your mind. When the pure energy passes through the film strip, it is thus colored by it and thus its vibration is lowered.

How do you create the film strip? You do so by accepting certain illusions, and these beliefs are perversions of the pure qualities of one of the seven rays. For example, one of the characteristics of the first ray is power. This is a pure creative power that seeks to raise all life. Yet when you look at earth, you can see that many people have perverted this pure form of power. They might use power to destroy other forms of life or to control them. Or they may use power to raise up themselves by putting others down.

So karma is made when you accept certain illusions, created by perverting the qualities of the seven rays. Which means that in order to balance the karma made in the past and stop making more karma, you need to overcome these illusions, so you can see and apply the pure qualities of the seven rays.

YOUR DIVINE PLAN

The ultimate goal of the path offered by the ascended masters is that you qualify for your ascension, which means you no longer have to come back into embodiment on earth. One of the requirements for ascending is that you balance karma. However, it is important to realize, that when your I AM Presence decided to send the Conscious You into embodiment, you did so for a positive purpose. You did not simply come here in order to make karma, balance karma and then leave. You came here to bring a gift of your spiritual light, that would help raise the earth and the material universe. So you really do not want to ascend until that purpose has been fulfilled.

The masters teach that each of us has several ascended masters who serve as our personal councilors. Before we come into embodiment, we meet with our councilors in order to formulate a specific plan for our next embodiment. This is often called our Divine plan. This plan is very specific and it outlines where we will be born, who will be our parents, who will be our children, what people we will marry and associate with in other ways, what education we might pursue and what kind of spiritual activities we will join.

The Divine plan is, of course, an outline, and it is very much subject to our free will. It is also based on the reality that we forget our Divine plan and thus have to rediscover it. However, many spiritual people have an intuitive sense that there is a specific purpose for our lives, that there are certain things we have to do, people we have to meet and lessons we have to learn. The more we increase our intuition (by clearing the four levels of our minds), the more we will get a sense of our Divine plan.

It is important to realize that each person's Divine plan is unique. Thus, it is not productive when spiritual people want to tell others how they should live their lives. You truly cannot know with your outer mind what is another person's Divine plan. And the reason is that your Divine plan is not something that you can be told—it truly is something that you must discover from within. This is just one reason why Jesus told us not to judge after appearances. It sometimes seems like other people are doing things that appear to be not right, but in many cases they have an intuitive sense that this is part of their Divine plans, and thus it really doesn't matter how it appears to an outsider. Let us look at some examples of this.

The Divine plan sets an overall focus for your present lifetime, and it very much depends on where you are at on your personal path towards your ascension. Here are some common scenarios:

- Some people have so much karma that they cannot realistically qualify for their ascensions in the present lifetime. Thus, their focus might be on balancing karma, which means they do not even have to be involved with spiritual teachings and activities. It might be more important for them to meet the people with whom they have karma. It may seem as if such people are not spiritual or that they often get into conflicts with others, yet they are doing precisely what they should be doing based on their Divine plans.

- Some people may be close to qualifying for the ascension, yet they still have a lot of karma to balance. Thus, their focus is on balancing karma in the fastest way possible. This will often lead them to spiritual teachings and techniques, and they feel a great urge to practice spiritual techniques very diligently. It may even be right for such people to withdraw from society and live in a retreat setting, at least for a while. Yet people who balance a lot of karma may also lead seemingly chaotic lives. They may have several spouses, several jobs or careers and they may move a lot, even from country

| 14 | *An ascended master perspective on karma*

to country. They are simply doing what it takes to encounter as many of their karmic connections as possible.

• Some people are close to qualifying for their ascensions, but in order to do so, the main task is not to balance karma but to express their unique gift. For such people it is not productive to withdraw from the world. They need to be engaged with other people and with society, so they can express their light and their talents. Some of these people may still find a spiritual teaching, but many of these people are not involved with a spiritual movement, yet they are doing exactly what they should be doing in order to bring their gift to society.

• Some people are not yet ready to make their ascensions, but they are ready to engage in the spiritual path in a way that goes beyond traditional religion. Thus, the main focus for such people is to study spiritual teachings, so they can increase their understanding.

• Some people may be close to their ascensions, but whether they can actually make their ascension at the end of this lifetime depends on them working out the hang-ups in their own psyches. Thus, for these people the main focus is not spiritual teachings but personal psychology. They may study spiritual teachings and practice techniques, or they may engage in various forms of therapy. They may even become therapists or healers themselves, because seeking to help others heal is the way to their own healing. Such people are seeking to work through the layers in their own psyches, until they uncover the one illusion that is at the bottom of the separate self. At that moment, they will experience a major shift, as they are now free to focus on bringing their gift.

These are just some among the many possible scenarios, but they illustrate that we really cannot judge other people, and we really should not judge ourselves. Many spiritual people have the potential to make much progress in this lifetime, but it requires us to go through several phases. For example, many people start their lives by being involved with karmic situations. Only after some time do they find the spiritual path, and in the beginning it is right for them to set aside everything else in order to study a spiritual teaching and practice techniques. In other words, for a time it is right to withdraw from society.

Yet after you have balanced a certain amount of karma and resolved certain conditions in your psychology, it is now right to go out into society. You are now ready to express your gift, and this often cannot be done if you continue to withdraw from the world.

Many spiritual people have made the decision to get their karma and their psychological wounds over with as quickly as possible. That is why we sometimes lead very untraditional and seemingly chaotic lives. We often can't give a rational explanation for why we have to do certain things that seem crazy to family members. But the underlying reason is that we have to do this in order to balance karma or in order to confront certain hang-ups in our psychology.

By becoming more aware of the path offered by the ascended masters, you can more quickly balance karma, learn your lessons and resolve your psychology. Which means you can come to a point, where you look back at your life and realize, that you did exactly what you needed to do in order to move forward with your Divine plan. And now you are ready to step up to a much more fulfilling and enjoyable level.

The conclusion is that your Divine plan is more like a river. It does not stand still, and in order to fulfill your highest potential, you have to be willing to flow with the river as it winds its way towards the ocean of self.

THE ASCENSION: THE ULTIMATE GOAL

As said before, the ascension is the ultimate goal of the spiritual path for us humans. However, for you to qualify for the ascension, a number of requirements must be met. One of these is karma. The masters have said that in previous ages, it was necessary to balance 100% of your karma before you could ascend. However, a dispensation is now in place, which makes it possible to ascend with 51% of your karma balanced. There are several reasons why this dispensation was given.

In order to understand them, it is necessary to consider that the earth is currently in a transition phase between two spiritual periods or ages. As mentioned, the last 2,000 years is called the Age of Pisces and the next 2,000 years is called the Age of Aquarius. Such ages do follow the precession of the equinoxes, but the exact line that separates one age from the next cannot simply be determined by the movement of the stars. Everything on earth is subject to free will, and thus the shift to the next age will not happen until a critical mass of people shift their consciousness into the new mindset and thus produce a shift in the collective consciousness.

One reason for giving a dispensation that makes it easier to ascend is to help bring about the shift in the collective consciousness. When a person qualifies for the ascension, it creates a magnetic pull that lifts the collective consciousness. Jesus illustrated this when he said: "And I, if I be lifted up from the earth, will draw all men unto me."

Another point is that at the end of one age, there will be a certain amount of people who were meant to ascend in the old age. And if these people are not close to balancing 100% of their karma, then the dispensation to ascend with 51% balanced can obviously be their only realistic hope of ascending. And as mentioned above, it is indeed right for such people to be very goal-oriented and do anything necessary to reach the goal of balancing more than 51% of their karma.

Yet this does not mean that all spiritual people should be equally focused. For many it is not their time to ascend, or it is more important to balance 100% of their karma before they ascend. The masters teach that while you can indeed ascend with 51% balanced, you still have to balance any remaining karma. And it is harder to balance karma in the spiritual realm than here in embodiment. It is also possible that it is more important for you to focus on some of the other requirements for the ascension, instead of only thinking about balancing karma.

As mentioned before, you did not come here to make karma, balance karma and then ascend. You came here to learn and you came here

The Power of Self

to express your Divine gifts. Thus, unless it truly is your time to ascend in this transition phase from Pisces to Aquarius, you will not want to ascend until you have learned what you want to learn and given the gift you want to bring.

You cannot ascend if you are seeking to run away from anything on earth.

The simple fact is that although you can list certain outer requirements for the ascension – balancing karma, giving your gift – there is also an inner requirement. Let us say you fulfill all outer requirements and you are standing before the doorway that leads to the ascended state. If you walk through the doorway, you will be ascended, but before you can walk through, you must make a decision. And part of this decision is that you must be willing to leave the earth – and everything and everyone on it – behind forever.

So the question is: Are you ready to leave the earth behind forever, or is there still something you want to do or experience on this planet? Again, the ascension is *not* something that can or will be forced upon you. It is a choice you make, and you can only make it when you feel you have had enough of what life on this planet has to offer.

This does not mean that the ascension is a form of escape. You cannot ascend if you are seeking to run away from anything on earth. Thus, you must come to a point, where you have made peace with life on this planet. You are not seeking to run away from anything, you are embracing life in a positive way. Yet you nevertheless feel that you have experienced everything you want to experience, and thus you are truly ready to move on to a higher level.

The conclusion is that the real goal of the spiritual path is to come to that point, where you have made peace with life on earth and you have made peace with your own desires to experience or do something on this planet. You are no longer wanting to experience anything, and you are no longer wanting to change anything. You look at your sojourn on this planet with absolute peace, and you leave it behind with love, embracing a higher form of existence with that same love. Thus, inner peace can be said to be the true goal of the path offered by the ascended masters.

CHAPTER 15

UNDERSTANDING WHY YOU NEED THE ASCENDED MASTERS

The ascended masters teach that for a human being on earth, it is possible to be at 144 different levels of consciousness. The lowest level is one where people are extremely selfish and are absolutely convinced, that their perception is the only true one. The 144th level is the highest level possible before you ascend, and it is a level where all subjective perception filters have been transcended, so we see things the way they really are. Thus, there is a certain irony in that people with the lowest possible consciousness are convinced they have the highest possible status on earth, while in reality they are the most deceived. People at the 144th level are realistically humble, because they see the non-dualistic reality that all life is one.

When you fully understand the teaching about the 144 levels, you can explain any aspect of human behavior. For example, it is only when you go below the 48th level of consciousness, that it is possible to commit actions that are clearly selfish and spring from an insensitivity to other forms of life. The further you go down towards the lowest level, the more selfish you become, but not necessarily in an obvious way.

The lower levels of consciousness represent people who are completely blinded by the illusion of duality, which means they believe they have the right and the capacity to define what is good and evil. Obvious examples are some of the most ruthless dictators of history, such as Hitler, Stalin or Mao, who were firmly convinced that their world view was based on absolute reality, and thus it was perfectly justifiable to

| 15 | *Understanding why you need the ascended masters*

kill millions of people. In other words, the lower the consciousness, the more one is convinced that the ends can justify the means, and the more one is convinced that one viewpoint is right and that all other viewpoints are wrong.

UNDERSTANDING HOW BEINGS START THE PATH

The ascended masters teach that a new self-aware being does not come into embodiment at the lowest level. Instead, a newly created being comes into embodiment for the first time at the 48th level of consciousness. This is a level where you have two distinct options: You can start a path that leads you up towards the 96th level or you can start a path that leads you down towards the lowest level.

In order to illustrate this, let us again compare planet earth to a theater. In a theater performance you have a number of different roles that can be played. For example, you can be the hero, the villain, the merchant, the lover or any number of other roles. These many roles can be divided into two categories: those that lead you up and those that lead you down. Yet in order to fully understand the two categories, we need to take a closer look at the sense of self you have at the 48th level.

When a being first descends at the 48th level, it has a very localized or point-like sense of self. It sees itself as an individual being, and it sees that it is surrounded by other beings who have an individual will. It also sees that it lives in an environment made of "solid" matter, and it sees no direct connection between itself and matter. Yet here comes a very important distinction: A new being does not see itself as a disconnected or separate being. A new being has an inner, intuitive sense of being connected to something greater than itself. This "something" is the being's I AM Presence, but the being has no direct perception of the Presence; it has only an inner sense that it is connected to something that is real.

This connection is extremely important, because it gives the new being a unique frame of reference. The being senses that there is indeed something beyond its own mind, and that something is real in an ultimate sense. And this gives the being a frame of reference for evaluating what is going on inside its own mind. In other words, when you have the frame of reference of knowing there is something real outside your own mind, you can never be fully identified with the contents of your own mind. We can also say that when you take on a role in the theater of earth, you can never be fully identified with that role. You know you are more than the role, and thus you have the potential to transcend or step out of the role. You know you are not stuck in the role for the indefinite future.

This inner sense of connection to something beyond your own mind means you are open to a spiritual teacher. The ascended masters teach that when a new lifestream descends into embodiment for the first time, it is not simply thrown into the environment we currently see on earth and then left to sink or swim. On the contrary, a new lifestream first descends into a protected environment, where it is under the direct guidance of an ascended master. The stories of a lost paradise, found in so many religions, refer to this kind of environment, and one example is the story of the Garden of Eden.

A new lifestream first descends into a protected environment, where it is under the direct guidance of an ascended master.

The "God" in the Garden of Eden was the ascended master Lord Maitreya, and each of the trees represented certain spiritual initiations. You might remember that the "God" in Eden had told Adam and Eve (symbols for every lifestream) that they could eat of all of the fruits except one. Here is what this truly means.

THE IDEAL SCENARIO

A new lifestream finds itself under the guidance of an ascended master. The lifestream will ideally choose to engage in the path offered by the ascended masters. This path is designed to take the lifestream through

| 15 | *Understanding why you need the ascended masters*

seven levels of initiation, whereby the lifestream will rise from the 48th level of consciousness to the 96th level. The masters call this the "Path of the Seven Veils," because each of the seven levels can be seen as a veil that obscures your vision of the spiritual realm. When you pass the initiations on one level, you gain a clearer vision of the spiritual realm. You also become more aware of your co-creative abilities, and thus you move closer to manifesting the full power of Self.

The seven levels correspond to the seven spiritual rays. We earlier saw that the entire material universe is made from spiritual energy, that has been reduced in vibration by the reduction factors of the seven rays. When you start the path of initiation on the 48th level, you start out on the first ray, and you stay on it as your main ray until you reach the 54th level.

Yet for each level, there is an Alpha and an Omega. So on the 48th level, your Alpha is the first ray and your Omega is the first ray. On the 49th level your Alpha is the first ray and your Omega is the second ray—and so on. At the 55th level, the second ray becomes the Alpha, and you again go through the seven rays as the Omega.

This continues to the 96th level, where you have now come to know all of the seven rays, and you have hopefully attained a high level of integration of the rays. This means you have some mastery on all seven rays without having an unbalanced attainment on one of the rays. For example, you do not have the hallmark of a dictator, who is very strong on the first ray of power but does not have it balanced by the second ray of wisdom or the third ray of love.

This balance and integration means that at the 96th level, you are ready to take a special initiation. In the Garden of Eden story this initiation is symbolized by the "forbidden fruit."

UNDERSTANDING THE FORBIDDEN FRUIT AND THE FALL OF MAN

In the Garden of Eden story, the "God" (the spiritual teacher), had told Adam and Eve that they could eat all of the fruits of the garden, except one. This symbolizes that the initiates can partake of all of the initiations (fruits) of the seven rays.

The forbidden fruit represents a special initiation, and in the Garden of Eden story, Adam and Eve had been told that if they ate this fruit, they would surely die. You might also recall that the serpent tempted eve into eating the fruit by saying; "Thou shallt not surely die." Eve then ate the fruit, and did not die but was cast out of paradise. So did the God in the garden lie to Adam and Eve and was the serpent right? Well, that requires a more subtle understanding than what is found in the Bible.

As mentioned, the ascended master Lord Maitreya was the leader of the mystery school that was the basis for the Garden of Eden story. He has described the process of the fall in great detail in the book *Master Keys to Spiritual Freedom*. So what will be given here is the short version based on the 144 levels.

Let us begin by realizing that a new lifestream walking the path of the seven veils is by no means a saint. Such a being has a very localized sense of identity and is clearly focused on raising itself up by passing initiations and acquiring wisdom and skills. It is doing this as an individual being, and it may even have a sense of competition with other beings in the mystery school, seeking to do better than others or do well in the eyes of the teacher.

This is perfectly natural and it is allowed, because it is not what we normally call selfishness. It is truly a desire to do well as an individual being. Beings in a mystery school are in a group environment, very much like a sports team. Each member of a sports team is striving to perfect its own abilities, but they are still able to work together for the benefit of the team. So the process of increasing your individual abilities is the path of passing the initiations of the seven rays.

In the ideal scenario, a lifestream maintains, and even increases, its inner sense of being connected to something greater than itself. As it grows on the path, it ideally expands its sense of being connected to its teacher and to other students in its environment. This inner connection is based on the underlying reality, that any self-aware being is an extension of a greater being, which is an extension of a greater being—which

| 15 | *Understanding why you need the ascended masters*

in the end is an extension of the Creator. Thus, behind all surface appearances, the underlying reality is that all life is one.

A planet like earth is a cosmic unit, and all lifestreams who embody here are connected with an invisible web of life. Thus, whatever you do as an individual being, will inevitably affect the whole, and since you are part of that whole, it will also affect yourself. There is simply no way you can do something to another human being that will not have an effect on yourself.

We earlier compared planet earth to a theater with a number of roles. As long as you have an inner sense of connection to the whole, there are certain roles that you will not choose to play. Simply speaking, you would never chose to play the role of a villain, as a villain is a person who performs acts that seemingly benefit itself by violating others.

As we have just seen, it truly is not possible to perform an act that will hurt another and at the same time benefit yourself. All life is connected, so if you hurt any part of life, you will also hurt yourself. Now consider this subtlety: It is not possible to perform an act that hurts another without hurting yourself, but it is indeed possible to *believe* that you can perform an act that hurts another while benefitting yourself.

Yet how is it possible to believe in this illusion? Well, it is not possible while you see yourself as an individual being who is connected to a larger whole. As long as you are conscious of your connection to something outside your self, you will have an inner knowing that you are part of a whole. So in order to believe in the illusion, that you can raise yourself by putting another down, you must enter into a different state of consciousness, a different sense of self.

This is precisely what the ascended masters call the consciousness of separation—which is truly the "forbidden fruit." It is also what Jesus referred to as "death," meaning a state of spiritual death. For example, Jesus was once approached by a young man who wanted to follow him but asked permission to first bury his father. Jesus answered: "Let the dead bury their dead." Obviously, the people burying the father were not physically dead, so the logical conclusion is that Jesus considered them spiritually dead. That is why he said: "I am come that all might have life, and that more abundantly."

Now, you might ask: "Well, but why was the forbidden fruit in the garden in the first place?" The reason is that the forbidden fruit is an inevitable companion of free will. The Creator knows that the only way we can grow in self-awareness is by having a will that is completely free. We grow by making choices and seeing the consequences of them. Yet there is only one way to give us free will, and that is to give us the opportunity to make any choice we can imagine. If there are certain choices we cannot make, then our will is not truly free, and then we cannot grow to the ultimate level of self-awareness.

The Creator knows that the only way we can grow in self-awareness is by having a will that is completely free. We grow by making choices and seeing the consequences of them.

Let us now return to the idea that there are two basic categories of choices we can make. One is choices based on the self-awareness that we are part of a whole, and the other is choices based on the self-awareness that we are separate, disconnected beings. How can we make the latter type of choices? We cannot do so while we maintain the self-awareness that we are connected beings. So we must make a shift into seeing ourselves as disconnected beings, and that means our former sense of self will die, and a new self is born.

The ascended masters are by no means saying that the Garden of Eden story is correct in every detail, but they do say the symbolism is useful. So the God in the garden was indeed truthful, when se said that if you eat of the forbidden fruit, you – meaning the sense of self as a connected being – will surely die. Instead, you will turn into a being who sees itself as a separate, disconnected being. You will die as a spiritual being and be reborn as a disconnected being. A separate being is spiritually

| 15 | *Understanding why you need the ascended masters*

dead, because it no longer sees itself as part of the web of life. Instead of being part of the one life, it is apart from life. How exactly does this happen?

UNDERSTANDING THE SUBTLETY OF THE SERPENTINE LOGIC

As long as you see yourself as a being who is connected to a larger whole, you know that ultimate reality is found not only outside your own mind, but in a higher realm than the material. When you make the shift into seeing yourself as a separate being, you lose this inner frame of reference. Thus, you now become susceptible to the illusion symbolized by the serpent in the Garden of Eden. This illusion makes you believe that you are fully capable of defining ultimate reality inside your own mind and that you do not need a frame of reference from the spiritual world. You can rely on an authority in this world (such as a religion, a political philosophy or scientific materialism) or you can rely on the belief that you can personally define what is real.

Take note of the subtle difference. Even if you follow a religion or spiritual guru, you are still relying on a frame of reference from this world. In fact, even the teachings of the ascended masters can become an outer frame of reference, once they are expressed in words. According to the masters, what is needed in order for us to walk the path that leads from the 48th to the 96th level, is that we do not rely on a frame of reference from this world. Instead, we expand our inner frame of reference, which is a direct, intuitive connection to our higher beings and the ascended masters. There is a fundamental difference between being told what to do by an external teacher or receiving intuitive guidance from an inner teacher. And the main difference is that the inner teacher cannot be manipulated by your own ego or by an external authority. And that is why the inner teacher is the only way to escape the illusions created in your own mind. (Another important aspect is that an ascended teacher needs nothing from you and thus has no self-interest.)

The Power of Self

In the Garden of Eden story, it is said that the serpent told Eve that if she ate the forbidden fruit, she would not die, but would become "as a God, knowing good and evil." This is a symbol for the fact, that when you see yourself as a separate being, you indirectly think that you are as a God, and that you have the ability and the authority to define what is good and evil, real and unreal. That is why a dictator can truly believe, that he has the right to define certain people as subhumans, meaning it is perfectly justifiable to exterminate them. In other words, the consciousness of the serpentine mind, the dualistic state of mind, can literally justify anything. In contrast, as long as you see yourself as connected to a larger reality, there are some things that you simply know are not justifiable, such as mass murder.

The forbidden fruit is a symbol for seeing yourself as a separate being; you indirectly think that you are as a God, and that you have the authority to define what is good and evil, real and unreal.

We could also say that as long as the Self sees itself as a part of a larger whole, it has some access to the powers of the whole. It can serve as an open door for the power of Spirit to flow into this world. Once you step into a disconnected self, you lose access to this power. Thus, you can only use the energy that is already in the material frequency spectrum. And that means you are now in constant competition with other people. The spiritual energy is infinite, but the material energy is finite. When people have to fight over a finite amount, the inevitable result is a struggle, as world history clearly demonstrates. So in order to truly unlock the powers of Self, you need to get back to seeing yourself as a Self that is part of the whole and has access to the infinite power of Spirit.

| 15 | *Understanding why you need the ascended masters*

HOW THE FALL HAPPENED

Let us now return to the ideal scenario. A new being starts at the 48th level, engages in the path of taking the initiations of the seven rays, and thus it rises towards the 96th level, where it has attained some mastery on all seven rays. What exactly does this mean? Well, we have said earlier, that everything in the material universe is made from the energies of the seven rays. Thus, whenever you take an action of any kind, there are two elements involved: driving force and direction. You can take an action only by using energy. You cannot produce this energy, but your mind can be an open door for the energies of one or more of the seven rays. Thus, you take an action by applying a direction to the energy of one or more of the rays.

There are two ways to use energy: for selfless purposes and selfish purposes. Which means that when a human being does something selfish, it is still done with the energies of one of the seven rays. However, selfish actions are possible only by perverting one or more of the rays, and then using this perverted energy to raise up the separate self. Each ray has a certain vibration. When you seek to raise all life, the energy you use stays above a certain level, meaning it can rise back to the spiritual realm, where it will be multiplied and sent back to you. When you act selfishly, you lower the energy below the critical level, meaning the misqualified energy must stay in the material spectrum, where it becomes a burden that you carry with you until you raise its vibration.

In the ideal scenario, a lifestream would learn how to use the energies of the seven rays without making the choice to do so for selfish purposes. However, this would not mean, that the lifestream knew nothing about the perversions. A lifestream would indeed learn about the perversions of the seven rays; it simply would not choose to use these lower energies. Therefore, it would continue to climb towards the 96th level without going below the 48th level.

In the ideal scenario, a lifestream would reach the 96th level, and at this level it would be ready to pass the initiation represented by the forbidden fruit, the serpentine consciousness. In other words, the lifestream would be ready to see through the illusion that its mastery of the seven rays has turned it into a god who has the right to define how it uses its creative powers.

At this point, the lifestream would be well-prepared for this initiation, because it has now learned about the positive qualities and the perversions of the seven rays. Thus, it is unlikely that the lifestream would lose its inner sense of connection, die as a connected being and be reborn as a separate being.

In other words, the ideal scenario is designed specifically to make it easier for a lifestream to pass the inevitable initiation (and temptation) of the serpentine mind, the duality consciousness. Thus, the lifestream could confront the serpent without being deceived into believing that it really has the capacity and the right to define its own reality inside its own mind. It could, so to speak, eat the forbidden fruit without dying.

However, take note that because lifestreams have completely free will, it is possible that a lifestream can choose to eat the forbidden fruit before it has reached the 96th level. This means that the lifestream has not yet learned about the perversions of all of the seven rays, and thus it is virtually inevitable, that the lifestream will be deceived by one of these perversions, thinking it is not a perversion but a virtue or a reality.

So the forbidden fruit was forbidden only for those students who had not yet reached the 96th level. Which means that the fall happened because some students were deceived into thinking they were ready before the teacher had approved them to be ready. In other words, they thought they knew better than the teacher.

When a lifestream eats the forbidden fruit before being ready, it will surely die as a connected being and be reborn as a separate self. As such, it will have no inner connection to a larger reality, which means it will no longer be open to a spiritual teacher. Instead, it has become its own teacher, and it can no longer learn in the environment of the mystery school. Thus, it is "cast out of paradise" and must now learn without the direct assistance of a spiritual teacher. Instead, it will learn by experiencing the consequences of the choices it makes as a separate being. This is what the ascended masters call the "School of Hard Knocks."

| 15 | Understanding why you need the ascended masters

Instead of learning from the guidance of an enlightened teacher, you now learn by experiencing the material circumstances that correspond to your mental images. And since those mental images are based on the illusion that you are a separate being struggling against other beings, against the matter world or even against God, your life inevitably becomes an ongoing struggle. This is what the Buddha called the "Sea of Samsara." The Buddha also said that the first noble truth is that life is suffering, but the deeper meaning is that life is suffering when you are in the consciousness of separation.

Instead of learning from the guidance of an enlightened teacher, you now learn by experiencing the material circumstances that correspond to your mental images.

So the conclusion is that as you walk the path between the 48th and the 96th level of consciousness, you can at any moment choose to partake of the serpentine temptation. If you do, you will then fall below the 48th level, and the level to which you fall will correspond to the level to which you had climbed before you fell. If you fell at the 58th level, you would fall ten places below the 48th, namely to the 38th level. If you fell at the 96th level, you would fall to the first level.

This fact partly explains why some of the worst dictators in history have had an uncanny ability to mesmerize people and get others to follow them blindly. A person with this ability fell at a high level of the path, and thus he or she can easily persuade those who are currently at a lower level than where the leader fell. If you fall at the 96th level, you can outsmart and overpower most people at a lower level.

The Power of Self

A CLOSER LOOK AT THE SERPENTINE MIND

Before we move on, let us look at what it means to take the serpentine initiation or temptation before you are ready for it. We have said that the path between the 48th and the 96th level of consciousness is a path of raising your individual self. This means your responsibility is to raise yourself, and you have no responsibility for other people.

Yet when you look at the serpent in the Garden of Eden story, it is clear that the serpent was aggressively seeking to influence Eve. Thus, the serpentine consciousness represents the temptation to seek to actively influence the free will of other beings. Take note of a basic fact. Every self-aware being is an individual being and is endowed with an individual will that is completely free. You truly do have the right to make any choice you want—because the law of God will make sure, that you will experience the consequences of your own choices.

The serpentine consciousness represents the temptation to seek to actively influence the free will of other beings.

Yet it is one thing for you to make any choice you want, even if your choices affect other people. It is a fundamentally different thing for you to seek to influence the choices that other people make. This may seem subtle, but it is one of the most important points for spiritual people to understand. The reason is that unless you have uncompromising respect for free will – your own and that of others – you simply cannot avoid falling for the serpentine temptation.

As an illustration of this, consider that a person decides to kill someone else. This is clearly an act that affects the person who is being killed. Yet it is still an act for which the perpetrator is personally responsible. So if the perpetrator is discovered, he or she will be held accountable by society. Now consider that the perpetrator decides to kill another person. Yet instead of doing it himself, he manages to manipulate a third

| 15 | *Understanding why you need the ascended masters*

person into killing the other person. This act of manipulating a person's mind is fundamentally different from killing a person's body. It is a direct violation of the person's free will, and it is precisely this kind of mind manipulation that is the goal of the serpentine consciousness.

WHAT TYPE OF EXPERIENCES DO YOU WANT?

Let us again return to the concept that the earth is a theater, and there are many roles you can play. As long as you see yourself as a connected being, there are some roles you simply will not choose to play. Thus, we might say that when you have the self-awareness that you are part of a whole, there are some experiences you cannot have on earth. For example, you cannot have the experience of being a great warrior, who is skilled in battle and able to defeat any opponent.

It is quite possible that a lifestream can look at earth and decide that it wants to have the experience of being a warrior who is fighting an enemy. In order to have this experience, the lifestream must then die as a connected being and be reborn into a new self-awareness as a separate being. Only by doing this, can the lifestream believe that it can kill others without harming itself.

Now, take note of a subtle but all-important distinction. Playing the role of a warrior is not a violation of the free will of others. If a number of lifestreams make the choice that they want to experience what it is like to fight others, then they are all choosing to play certain roles. And obviously, you cannot be a warrior unless there is someone to fight. So if both sides are making the same choice, then none of them are violating the free will of others. It may seem as if an army attacking another country is violating the free will of the inhabitants of that country. Yet if those inhabitants have also chosen to be in the consciousness of separation, then they are inviting an attack—even if they are not consciously aware of this.

So what we now see is that when you go below the 48th level of consciousness, you do go into a frame of mind, where you perform selfish acts. And you are indeed blinded by an illusion, because you believe you

The Power of Self

can kill others without harming yourself. Yet this illusion is *not* the serpentine mind. It is simply ignorance.

The serpentine mind is a different form of ignorance, which we might call willful or sophisticated ignorance. The serpentine mind does not simply make you believe you can harm others without harming yourself. The serpentine mind makes you believe that your selfish actions are justified according to some ultimate reality.

As a historical example, take the Christian crusades. Here we have a group of people who claim to be followers of Christ. And of course, Christ told us to turn the other cheek, do unto others and to not resist evil. Yet the crusaders had managed to interpret the teachings of Christ in such a way, that it seemed as if they were doing God's work by killing Muslims (who thought they were doing God's work by killing Christians).

The serpentine mind does not simply make you believe you can harm others without harming yourself. The serpentine mind makes you believe that your selfish actions are justified.

Now compare this to some of the warrior groups we have seen throughout history, such as the vikings or the hordes of Attila the Hun. Both the huns and the crusaders attacked cities and mercilessly massacred men, women and children, stealing any loot they could find. Yet the huns and the vikings did this because of a desire for plunder or honor in battle, whereas the crusaders claimed they were doing this to further the cause of Christ, the cause of God.

Now look at the difference in mindset. A viking simply wants to engage in battle and has no sophisticated philosophical overlay that seeks to justify his actions. A crusader, however, has a philosophical framework, that in his eyes makes it not only justifiable to kill other people, but even makes him believe he will be rewarded for this in heaven. The crusaders believed, that if you died on a crusade, you were sure to go to

| 15 | *Understanding why you need the ascended masters*

heaven. And this justification is precisely the serpentine mind. In reality, it is based on the reasoning that an earthly authority has the right to define what is good and evil. Thus, a medieval pope could override the direct words of Christ and define that it was evil to kill another Christian, but it was good to kill a Muslim. The serpentine mind always divides, and in this case it divided humans into two categories, thus denying the deeper reality that all life is one.

As you walk the path from the 48th to the 96th level, you are supposed to learn how to use the positive qualities of the seven rays to raise up yourself and gain mastery over your own mind. An essential part of this initiation is that you fulfill the requirement described by Jesus: "Be ye wise as serpents, harmless as doves." This means you learn that while it is perfectly legitimate to use the positive qualities of the seven rays in order to raise yourself or raise all life, it is never legitimate to use the seven rays to influence the free will of other people. You learn that it is never acceptable to in any way – subtle or overt – force the will of another being. You can seek to persuade or inspire by example, but you never seek to force or manipulate.

Yet as you walk this path, you are constantly faced with the serpentine temptation, and here is how it works. Say you are working on the fifth ray of truth. You come to appreciate the positive qualities of truth, and it becomes very obvious to you, that all of the problems on earth spring from the fact that people do not see the truth but believe in various lies.

The serpent will now whisper in your ear, that if only all other people could be made to accept the truth that you see, then all of the problems of the world could be solved. If you are interested in this, the serpent will present the next temptation, namely that it is indeed desirable – even for God – to solve all of the problems on this planet. And if you again do not rebuke the tempter, there will be the third layer of temptation, namely that in order to fulfill God's own purpose, surely it is both justifiable and necessary to apply some level of force in order to get other people to accept the ultimate truth that you possess.

This very easily leads to the belief that there is only one true thought system – be it religious, political or materialistic – and that it is justifiable to force people to accept it. The ends of furthering God's ultimate cause surely justifies the means of forcing other people—for their own good.

The deeper reality is that you have an inherent sense that free will is individual and that you have no right to force the free will of another human being. Yet the serpentine mind presents you with a very subtle justification – the serpent was the most subtil of all the animals in the garden – for seeking to actively influence the free will of others. And the way to do this is to use the qualities of one or more rays in a way that is not based on love but on force. It is out of this mindset that the worst atrocities on this planet have sprung. For when you are fighting for the ultimate cause, there is no action that cannot be justified. Killing millions of men, woman and children in gas chambers is simply a necessary step towards your vision of a final solution.

EARTH IS BELOW THE IDEAL SCENARIO

In order to complete our understanding of current conditions, we need to realize that planet earth is today far below the ideal scenario. As mentioned before, in the distant past several waves of lifestreams took embodiment on earth without falling into duality. Yet at some point, a number of lifestreams did fall into duality. And since then, the earth has been a schoolroom that does not only contain lifestreams that are new on the path.

Let us return to the question of why the serpent was in the Garden of Eden. We can now see that there are two layers of understanding. In its most general sense, the serpent represents the duality consciousness. This is the temptation to use your powers to manipulate others in order to raise up the separate self. You can do this only by believing that you can define reality, so that your selfish actions seem to have some ultimate validity and justification. In other words, this state of mind allows you to commit selfish actions while feeling fully justified in doing so.

| 15 | *Understanding why you need the ascended masters*

Yet a more specific definition sees the serpent as a symbol for lifestreams who had already entered the duality consciousness before they took embodiment on earth. This might have happened in a previous lifetime here on earth, but since that previous age where the first lifestreams fell, this planet has gone through a major shift. Instead of being a schoolroom adapted to new lifestreams, earth has become a sort of second chance for lifestreams who have fallen in other settings. This might be on other planets in the material universe, but it could also be lifestreams who fell in a previous sphere.

As mentioned before, there have been six previous spheres, and from the fourth sphere onwards, some beings have fallen in every sphere. Some of these fallen angels or fallen beings have been allowed to embody on earth, and they are truly the more dominant leaders in world history. Yet take note of one simple fact. It may seem harsh that new lifestreams are mixed with fallen lifestreams. Yet the new lifestreams were created with this in mind, and the ascended teachers did everything they could to prevent new lifestreams from falling. And even today, the ascended masters are doing everything they can to get any fallen lifestream back to the only true path that leads up from below the 48th level of consciousness.

WALKING THE SPIRITUAL PATH TODAY

What we have seen now is that the earth is currently far below the original vision of the Elohim, and thus it is far more difficult to follow the spiritual path while you are in physical embodiment on this planet. This does not mean it is impossible, as has been proven by many beings who started out like the rest of us but who are today ascended masters. Nevertheless, it is important to understand, that every aspect of life and society has been influenced in subtle ways by the serpentine consciousness, the consciousness that seeks to justify selfish motives by camouflaging them as benevolent or necessary.

What does this mean in practical terms? It means that all of us are confronted with the serpentine mind, no matter what level of the spiritual path we are at right now. So an integral part of walking the spiritual path is to learn to recognize the serpentine consciousness and see through its lies. The masters call this "Christ discernment."

How can this be done? Well, you cannot outsmart the serpentine mind by using the serpentine mind. As Albert Einstein said: "You cannot solve a problem with the same state of consciousness that created the problem." In fact, a subtle truth is that you cannot actually defeat the serpentine mind. Because in the serpentine mind, there are always two opposites, such as good and evil. To the serpentine mind, it seems that good can triumph over evil, but the Christ mind sees that both dualities are created in relation to each other and both are unreal. Thus, the more you resist what you see as evil, the more you trap yourself in a dualistic struggle that can never have any ultimate outcome.

The basic truth about the serpentine mind is that it forms a selective perception filter. Once you step into a self created through the serpentine mind, there are certain aspects of reality that you simply cannot see. The reason is that your separate self was created specifically to filter out those aspects of reality, that might challenge the actions of the separate self. And by filtering them out, the separate self can always justify its actions—because you cannot see what challenges your actions. We could also say that your perception filter makes it seem like some people are good and some are evil, and thus you think it is justifiable to kill the evil people in order to further a good cause. Yet in reality, this only keeps you trapped in the mindset where you are always fighting something.

So what is the way out? Well, the serpentine mind makes you believe, that you have the right and the capacity to define what is good and evil. And as long as you believe this, you can never escape the serpentine illusion. Why not? Because as long as you believe that your definition of good and evil is ultimately right, you will always think that you have to be on the side of good and that you have to fight evil. Thus, you cannot escape the struggle until you win the final victory over evil. Yet as history has abundantly proven, there will never be a final victory over evil, for the very act of fighting one evil creates the resistance (karma) that forms the next appearance of evil. So you are always fighting some appearance

| 15 | *Understanding why you need the ascended masters*

of evil, as Don Quixote was fighting the windmills. The reason is that it is your own perception filter that creates the appearances of evil.

The only real way out is to move back towards that original state, where you see yourself as a being who is connected to something beyond your personal mind. This can then become your lifeline, a frame of reference, that you can use to gradually raise yourself above the serpentine illusions of your separate self. And this is precisely what the ascended masters offer us through the path of the seven rays.

This path can be followed by anyone, even people who are below the 48th level. Yet it is indeed much harder to follow the path when you are below the 48th level, and the reason is that you are still believing in the illusion, that you can define reality from inside your own mind. Once you step behind this veil of duality, your mind becomes like quick-sand.

The ascended masters are the lifeline sent by God to help all of us escape the human enigma, the quicksand of our separate selves.

You probably know that if you fall into quick-sand, the more you move, the more you will sink. The more you think you can get out of the duality consciousness on your own, the more deeply you will go into illusion. How do you survive falling into quicksand? You must lie still until someone can throw you something you can grab on to and use as a fixed point to pull yourself out. Likewise, once you step into the mental quicksand of the serpentine mind, anything you do will only cause you to sink deeper. You must learn to still the mind so much, that you can receive a lifeline from beyond your own mind, and then you can use it to pull yourself up towards higher levels of awareness.

The ascended masters are the lifeline sent by God to help all of us escape the human enigma, the quicksand of our separate selves. They have been in the quicksand themselves, and they have walked the path of initiation that leads you out of it. Today, they are offering us the same time-tested, proven path.

Of course, you have free will, and the ascended masters will always respect it. If you need to continue to believe, that you are capable of getting out of the duality consciousness by your own powers, the masters will patiently stand back and wait until the hard knocks you produce will cause you to decide, that you have had enough of this path. And the moment you do open your mind and heart to the true inner path of initiation, the ascended masters will be ready to not only throw you a lifeline, but to multiply your own efforts to pull yourself up higher. It truly is a wonderful path of initiation, and once you walk it, you will personally experience the love from the ascended masters, a love that is beyond anything you can experience on earth.

PART FIVE

INTRODUCING THE SEVEN RAYS

CHAPTER 16

INTRODUCTION TO THE SEVEN RAYS

As we have seen, anything you do is done with energy, specifically the energy of the seven spiritual rays. Thus, in order to unlock the full creative power of Self, you need to have mastery on each of the seven rays. Likewise, anything you have done in the past was done with the energy from the seven rays. So the way to balance karma and become free from the past is to invoke the energies of the seven rays. Karma is made by qualifying the energies of a particular ray with a lower vibration, and the natural way to balance it is to invoke the pure energy of that ray. This higher energy can requalify or transmute the lower energy.

We have also seen that each ray has certain characteristics or properties. Understanding these will help you express a particular ray without misqualifying its energy. Seeing through all perversions of a ray is also the only way to stop making karma by misqualifying the energies of a ray. So all in all, getting to know the seven rays is a major key to personal and spiritual growth. The creative power of Self comes from the seven rays, so learning about them is an obvious way to accelerate your personal growth.

Obviously, all people have already attained some familiarity and mastery with the seven rays in this and previous lifetimes. Yet by becoming more consciously away of the rays, you can learn to draw upon the experiences and momentum stored in your causal body. You might discover that you have a strong momentum on one ray or that you are lacking momentum on another ray. If you find that you are currently working on a particular ray, you will also have some feel for where you are at on the path from the 48th to the 96th level of consciousness.

This book is the first in a series of books, and it is meant to be an introduction to the path of the seven rays offered by the ascended masters. The second book in the series will give a more thorough description of the seven rays, including teachings given directly by the seven Chohans. It will also contain a special exercise for invoking the light of the seven rays over a period of time. Completing this exercise will give you a much better intuitive sense of which ray or rays you might be working with at this stage of your personal path. You can then use that to select among the following books in the series, for which each book is dedicated to an in-depth study of one ray. The purpose of this chapter is to give a brief introduction of the seven rays, so that you can begin to get a feel for the rays and their qualities.

THE CHARACTERISTICS OF A RAY

Each of the following sections will help you get to know a ray. You will, for example, learn the color of the light of each ray, which is important for learning to visualize the light of a ray flowing through your mind. The colors you will be given correspond to the colors of visible light, but the actual colors of a spiritual ray are more ethereal or transparent. The colors are very pure and have an almost electric or vibrant quality.

You will also learn the three main masters who serve on each ray. They are:

- **The Elohim.** This is the master who is in charge of releasing the creative energies of a ray into the material frequency spectrum. We might say the Elohim is the creative director for a ray. You call to the Elohim in order to increase the flow of energy on a particular ray.

- **The Archangel.** This is the master who is in charge of passing on the energies of a ray from the level of the Elohim to our level. In other words, the Archangel steps down the vibration of the light so it can actually do something in our spectrum. For example, you might call on an Archangel to protect and seal your energy field or to bring healing.

- **The Chohan**. This is the master who serves as the main teacher for the ray. Thus, you call on the Chohan to help you learn the positive qualities of a ray and to help you transcend the perversions of a ray.

THE RAYS AND THE CHAKRAS

You are probably already aware that you have an energy field around your physical body. However, it is important to understand the actual relationship between the body and your energy field, or aura. As we have seen, everything in the material realm is made from higher energies that have been lowered in vibration. This means that some of the things we were taught in school simply are not correct.

For example, you probably saw a teacher take a bar magnet and hold it under a piece of paper while sprinkling iron filings on top of the paper. As if by magic, the iron filings organized themselves into a wavy pattern by aligning themselves with the invisible magnetic field. You were probably then told that this is because a magnet produces an invisible energy field around itself.

This image is out of alignment with the theory of relativity and quantum physics. The correct image is that the magnet does not produce the field, but that the field produces the magnet. In other words, the physical magnet is the most dense part of a larger energy field. Adjusting your mental image based on this realization is a key to unlocking your creative power.

Your physical body does have an energy field around it, but the body does not produce the field. Your physical body is the most dense part of the larger energy field made up of your four lower bodies, namely the identity body, the mental body, the emotional body and the physical body. So the physical body is alive and has energy to take action because it is receiving a stream of spiritual energy, which is stepped down in vibration through the three higher bodies.

16 | Introduction to the seven rays

This stepping down of vibration happens through seven centers in the energy field, often called chakras. You might think of them as portals between the spiritual realm and the material realm. The chakras are a kind of two-way communication device, meaning that you receive energy and knowledge through the chakras and your I AM Presence receives impressions and experiences back from you.

Image 16 - Chakras in their purified form

Each of the seven main chakras corresponds to one of the seven rays. The chakras are aligned along the spinal column, as depicted in Image 16.

In order to increase your awareness of and mastery on a particular ray, you use its corresponding chakra. For example, there is a chakra located over your throat area, and it is appropriately called the throat chakra. This chakra corresponds to the first ray, and the chakra is also called your power center. So if you desire to increase your power, you need to become more conscious of your throat chakra and how to use it to express power. This is part of what you do when you invoke spiritual light by using the spoken word.

A chakra is meant to be an open door for the energies of a particular ray. Yet when you misqualify the energies of a ray, the lower energies will begin to accumulate in its corresponding chakra. Thus, the chakra will gradually become clogged, and the lower energies will block higher energies from streaming through the chakra. The lower energies prevent the chakra from spinning in its natural way, and thus the chakra cannot carry or transmit as much energy. Many people have so little energy flowing through their chakras, that it severely restricts their creative powers. Thus, an essential key to unlocking the power of Self is to purify and balance the chakras.

In the second book in this series, you will be given an exercise for invoking the light of the spiritual rays over a seven month period. This exercise is designed to help you tune all of your chakras. (You can begin this exercise at any time by using the decrees found on transcendencetoolbox.com) As you go through the exercise for a particular ray, the energy you invoke will clear away the blocks from a chakra. Getting to know the positive qualities of a ray and seeing the perversions will help you transcend the incorrect beliefs that cause you to misqualify energy through a chakra. These beliefs are like glass pieces in the chakra that color the light with a lower vibration.

Please take note that there are many spiritual teachings that talk about chakras, and you may already be familiar with some of them. Various teachings give various colors for the seven chakras, and they might be different from those given here. Yet please do not be concerned about this. The colors used in this book are simply the colors of the spiritual ray that corresponds to each chakra.

INTRODUCING THE FIRST RAY

Color of the first ray: Electric blue
Corresponding chakra: Throat chakra
Elohim of the first ray: Hercules and Amazonia
Archangel and Archeia of the first ray: Michael and Faith
Chohan of the first ray: Master MORE, also known as El Morya, Morya, Master M, M, or Bapu.

Pure qualities of the first ray

Traditionally seen as the ray of power and will, yet from a deeper understanding the first ray represents the creative drive. This is the desire for self-expression, a willingness to experiment, even when the outcome of the experiment cannot be known ahead of time. Also a willingness to flow with life and learn from every experience. The first ray gives rise to the sense that everything matters, that life is exciting and that the individual truly can make a positive difference. The first ray is also the key to your willingness to work for raising the whole, instead of raising only yourself.

The Power of Self

Perversions of the first ray

The perversion of the creative will is a fear of the unknown, which is expressed as a will to abuse power in order to control one's circumstances, including other people. There is a fear of engaging in activities where the outcome cannot be predicted or guaranteed, which obviously stifles creativity. People with perverted first ray qualities are often engaged in a variety of power games with other people, all based on the desire to control the outcome. They may also be very critical or condemnatory towards those who do not conform to their view of life.

A perversion of the first ray qualities leads to an attempt to quell the very life force itself, which always points towards self-transcendence, and instead protect the separate self and what it thinks it can own in this world. This can lead to a sense of ownership over other people, which is one of the major sources of conflict on this planet. In milder cases, people have a fear of being creative and a sense of powerlessness, feeling that nothing really matters and that an individual cannot make a difference—thus, why even bother trying.

INTRODUCING THE SECOND RAY

Color of the second ray: Golden yellow
Corresponding chakra: Crown
Elohim of the second ray: Apollo and Lumina
Archangel and Archeia of the second ray: Jophiel and Christine
Chohan of the second ray: Lord Lanto

Pure qualities of the second ray

Traditionally seen as the ray of wisdom, illumination and self-knowledge. Yet at a deeper level, it is the ray that empowers you to see that the separate self is unreal and that separation is an illusion. It is through the second ray that you can experience the underlying reality that all life is one, because nothing can be separated from the omnipresent Creator. Openness to a higher understanding is also a quality of the second ray, as is the realization that there are many valid expressions of truth that all point to the same underlying reality of oneness.

Perversions of the second ray

The perversion of the second ray is the false wisdom, which thinks it knows everything or has an ultimate truth. This illusion is based on the

The Power of Self

central illusion of duality, namely that "reality" can divided into separate compartments and that the separate mind has the right and the ability to decide which is true and which is untrue. The perversions of the second ray can be seen in people who are absolutely sure that they are right – especially those who have become fanatical – and are willing to force others into compliance. Another perversion is intellectualism, where people can argue for or against any idea without ever going beyond the idea to a direct experience of the Spirit that is beyond words.

INTRODUCING THE THIRD RAY

Color of the third ray: Pink
Corresponding chakra: Heart
Elohim of the third ray: Heros and Amora
Archangel and Archeia of the third ray: Chamuel and Charity
Chohan of the third ray: Paul the Venetian

Pure qualities of the third ray

Traditionally, the third ray has been seen as the seat of love, compassion, charity, appreciation for beauty and selflessness. Yet, a deeper understanding is that the third ray is the seat of balance.

Love can be seen as the balancing force in life, the force that balances the two basic forces of creation, namely the outgoing (masculine or Father impulse) and the contracting (Feminine or Mother impulse). If these two forces are not balanced, there will be a tendency to take one of them towards the extreme. This means that anything which is created from imbalance will either be taken too far and thus blow apart, or it will not be taken far enough, and thus will not come to fruition and will eventually self-destruct through contraction.

The pure third ray qualities give you the ability to experience unconditionality, namely the one reality that is beyond the two extremes created by the dualistic mind. You can feel when something is dualistic, even though you may not yet have a detailed explanation. You simply sense that conditionality is not "right," because you experience the unconditional nature of God/reality in your heart.

Third ray qualities lead to a deep inner sense of oneness with all life, which gives rise to the ability to discern when something feels right (because it seeks to raise all life) or feels not right (because it seeks to raise one part of life while putting down another). It is through the third ray that you can know what is the right thing to do, even if you cannot yet explain why through the mind. It is also through the third ray qualities that you can sense when something is driven by a selfish impulse, which gives you the power to balance yourself.

Perversions of the third ray

The primary perversion of the third ray is a lack of balance, but this can be expressed in many subtle ways. One way is what many people call love, but which is really a possessive attempt to control others. In extreme forms, this can be expressed as hatred and the desire to punish or destroy those who refuse to be controlled. For example, many people fall in love but then begin to express a sense of ownership towards the person they claim to love.

Another perversion is the firm belief that the ends can justify the means, meaning that because a person loves this superior cause, it is justified to force or kill other people in order to further the cause. This perverted form of love has caused some of the worst atrocities in human history. Few people are harder to convince than those whose outlook on life has become unbalanced by fanaticism. It is what causes people to believe that in order to demonstrate their love for God, they have to kill other people.

INTRODUCING THE FOURTH RAY

Color of the fourth ray: Brilliant white
Corresponding chakra: Base
Elohim of the fourth ray: Purity and Astrea
Archangel and Archeia of the fourth ray: Gabriel and Hope
Chohan of the fourth ray: Serapis Bey

Pure qualities of the fourth ray

Traditionally, the fourth ray qualities are seen as purity, hope and self-discipline. Yet at a deeper level, the fourth ray is the interface between your Spirit and your physical body and the material world. The question asked at the level of the fourth ray is whether you will allow the material world to have power over your Spirit, so you limit your expression in this world.

The question is whether you believe the current conditions in the material world are real, permanent and unchangeable, or whether you are willing to unleash your creative power in order to accelerate the material world – the Mother element – beyond current conditions.

The fourth ray qualities empower you to avoid being trapped in the illusion that the appearances in the material world are real or permanent. You will thus be able to avoid being trapped in an endless cycle of seeking to fulfill lower, bodily, carnal or human desires. Instead, you will see this world as only a tool for your growth in self-awareness. This means you will effortlessly avoid activities that do not serve this purpose. Yet this has a deeper layer of understanding, as you will realize it is not a matter of avoiding all human or physical activities—it is a matter of spiritualizing them.

An important illusion to overcome on the spiritual path is the idea that there is a division between the spiritual and the material realm, between spiritual and material activities. Instead, you will be able to remain in oneness, making anything you do a spiritual activity. This will then serve to fulfill the purpose for taking embodiment in the first place, namely to accelerate the vibration of the entire material universe to a higher level, where it can become a permanent part of the spiritual realm.

Perversions of the fourth ray

Traditionally, the perversion is seen as impurity, and chaos. Yet at a deeper level, the perversion is the sense that current conditions are real, are the way they should be or are beyond your power to change. You begin to think this world is separated from the spiritual realm, perhaps even that it belongs to the devil and that you should leave it alone, not seeking to change it.

You might even believe you have no right to be a spiritual person in this world or that you have no right to express your spiritual powers in this world. Instead, you think you should accept current conditions and adapt to them. As the ultimate perversion, you might even believe that you are an entirely material being, a product of the material universe—that you have come from dust and that to dust thou shalt return. In this

The Power of Self

state of mind, there is, of course, no hope of acceleration to a higher state. Yet given that life itself is acceleration into More, this is a state of mind that Jesus called "death," meaning spiritual death.

INTRODUCING THE FIFTH RAY

Color of the fifth ray: Emerald green
Corresponding chakra: Third eye
Elohim of the fifth ray: Cyclopea and Virginia
Archangel and Archeia of the fifth ray: Raphael and Mother Mary
Chohan of the fifth ray: Hilarion

Pure qualities of the fifth ray

Traditionally, the fifth ray qualities are seen as truth and vision—yet vision of what? The fifth ray is the seat of single vision, as illustrated by Jesus in the remark: "If thine eye be single, thy whole body shall be full of light." The single-eyed vision is the Christ vision, which sees beyond duality. This is based on the realization that *any* expression of "truth" in the material world is less than the Spirit of Truth, and thus one must look beyond *any* outer expression in order to experience truth.

When one does, one sees that all divisions are unreal, and one sees the need to raise all life. This gives rise to Christ discernment, the ability to instantly identify and see through the lies of duality, that always seek to raise up one part of life by putting down another. This is exemplified in the situation in the Garden of Eden, where the Serpent said to Eve: "Thou shallt not surely die," thus inserting the element of doubt in her consciousness. The fifth ray qualities empower you to see through this serpentine logic. You can also see that all appearances in the material world are only temporary, and thus you can hold the immaculate vision for people or conditions to be transformed.

Perversions of the fifth ray

The perversions are lack of vision, a lack of ability to discern between the one non-dual Truth and the many dualistic "truths," leading to doubt and a sense of hopelessness or the sense that there is no truth. It is also the belief that there is only one truth, and that it is our truth. Also the sense that because we have the only truth, we are locked in a battle against those who promote another thought system, and that it is necessary and justified for us to criticize or even destroy their system. People who are critical of other people or ideas have perverted the fifth ray qualities. Another perversion is the tendency to say that if people do or believe certain things, they are bad people—failing to see beyond temporary appearances.

The Power of Self

INTRODUCING THE SIXTH RAY

Color of the sixth ray: Purple and gold
Corresponding chakra: Solar plexus
Elohim of the sixth ray: Peace and Aloha
Archangel and Archeia of the sixt ray: Uriel and Aurora
Chohan of the sixt ray: Lady Master Nada

Pure qualities of the sixth ray

Traditionally, the primary sixth ray quality is seen as peace, but it is a "peace that passeth understanding." Thus, it is an inner sense of being unmoved by the dualistic appearances that are pulling at one from all sides. It is the ability to stand in the midst of a raging conflict and feel the stillness within. It is the ability to feel the pull that seeks to draw you into an unbalanced expression of anger, yet you can remain centered and decide that you do not want to go there.

When you have this peace, you can then give truly selfless service, because you will intuitively work to bring harmony into every situation. And of course, harmony is the key to helping people see beyond the dualistic struggle and find common ground. A person with developed sixth ray qualities is always looking for common ground and has an ability (especially when the upper chakras are also pure) to draw people towards common ground.

Perversions of the sixth ray

The immediate perversion of the sixth ray qualities are anger and agitation, expressed as a very aggressive drive to force others to change or to punish those who resist. It is a non-peace that also passeth understanding, because there is no way to reason with a person who has perverted the sixth ray qualities. They act blindly on their feelings of rage, and they will time and time again do or say things they regret later. They will even do things that everyone knows are wrong, yet be completely blind to it at the moment.

Another perversion is what some see as peace, but it is truly passivity, the unwillingness to take a stand for anything. Thus, people with this perversion tend to act as victims, who can only react to external forces and refuse to take responsibility for their lives. There are also people who lose individuality and become part of a "mob mind" that acts blindly or blindly follows a strong leader. Another perversion is a blind sense that violence and warfare can provide viable solutions or that in some situations they are the only way to react, even justified ways to react.

The Power of Self

INTRODUCING THE SEVENTH RAY

Color of the seventh ray: Violet
Corresponding chakra: Seat of the soul or innocence chakra
Elohim of the seventh ray: Arcturus and Victoria
Archangel and Archeia of the seventh ray: Zadkiel and Amethyst
Chohan of the seventh ray: Saint Germain and Kuan Yin

Pure qualities of the seventh ray

Traditionally, the seventh ray qualities are seen as freedom, forgiveness and justice. Yet a deeper understanding is that the seventh ray is the seat of your playfulness, your willingness to approach life according to Jesus' statement: "Unless you become as a little child, ye shall in no way enter the kingdom."

When you embody the pure seventh ray qualities, you feel that you live in a world that is basically good, and you are here to express yourself and play with what is available. You are not worried or anxious about life or the future, and you trust that Spirit will protect you and that the Mother will nurture you. Thus, you feel a sense of bubbling freedom and a desire to experience what the world has to offer and to add to it through your own creative expression. You feel holy innocence.

Perversions of the seventh ray

The primary perversion of the seventh ray qualities is a tendency to take life very seriously. This can be expressed as a perversion of both freedom and justice, which combines into the sense that you live in a world where everything is a struggle, perhaps even a struggle against a force that is unjustly seeking to take away your freedom.

Take the old saying: "Laugh at the devil, and he runs away from you." There is a truth here, in the sense that if you take something too seriously, you give it power over you. Of course, one might say that there are many things in the world that are seeking to limit your freedom and that are unjust, so does that mean you should not take them seriously? Yet there is a balance, where one realizes the truth in another statement by Jesus: "Be ye wise as serpents, harmless as doves." There is a fine balance between being naive to the temporary conditions in the world and taking them so seriously that you think you cannot feel free until they are changed.

The extreme perversion of the seventh ray is the epic mindset, where one thinks the world is locked in an epic battle between good and evil, meaning that anything can be justified in the fight to destroy evil. This leads to complete insensitivity towards life, which has led to some of the worst examples of human cruelty. Yet, as with everything else, insensitivity towards others comes from an insensitivity towards oneself.

When you have perverted the seventh ray qualities, you tend to think that the problems in the world exist because other people don't take them as seriously as you do. As you overcome this imbalance, you realize that the conditions are still here because people take them too seriously, thus thinking the conditions of the material world have power over their spirits. In reality, we are all spiritual beings, and one of our ultimate tasks on earth is to demonstrate that we will not allow material conditions to limit our Spirits and their expression in this world. Allowing our higher selves to express themselves through us is the key to freedom, and it is the playfulness of the divine man-child, who knows he or she is one with the Father—and with God all things are possible.

ABOUT THE AUTHOR

Kim Michaels is a contemporary spiritual teacher and the author of many popular books about mystical Christianity, self-help and the universal path beyond the human ego and the duality consciousness. He writes with uncomplicated clarity about how to apply the timeless wisdom and gnosis from eastern and western spiritual masters to our daily challenges.

Kim has founded 4 inspirational spiritual websites:

transcendencetoolbox.com - practical spiritual tools for invoking light and transcending the limitations of the ego consciousness.

askrealjesus.com - original mystical teachings from Jesus.

ascendedmasteranswers.com - Ascended master answers about various topics.

ascendedmasterlight.com - Ascended master teachings and dictations about everything related to spiritual growth.

www.ingramcontent.com/pod-product-compliance
Lightning Source LLC
Chambersburg PA
CBHW070340100426
42812CB00005B/1376